FLORIDA STATE
UNIVERSITY LIBRARIES

APR 7 1998

TALLAHASSEE, FLORIDA

GARLAND STUDIES IN

THE HISTORY OF AMERICAN LABOR

edited by
STUART BRUCHEY
ALLAN NEVINS PROFESSOR EMERITUS
COLUMBIA UNIVERSITY

A GARLAND SERIES

THE AVAILABILITY OF WOMEN WORKERS

EFFECTS ON COMPANY LOCATION

VIRGINIA L. CARLSON

GARLAND PUBLISHING, INC.
A MEMBER OF THE TAYLOR & FRANCIS GROUP
NEW YORK & LONDON / 1997

Copyright © 1997 Virginia L. Carlson
All rights reserved

Library of Congress Cataloging-in-Publication Data

Carlson, Virginia L., 1959–
   The availability of women workers : effects on company location / Virginia L. Carlson.
       p.   cm. — (Garland studies in the history of American labor)
   Revision of the author's thesis (Ph.D.—Northwestern University, 1995)
   Includes bibliographical references and index.
   ISBN 0-8153-3009-X (alk. paper)
   1. Industrial location—Effect of labor market on—Illinois—Chicago Metropolitan Area. 2. Women—Employment—Illinois—Chicago Metropolitan Area. I. Title. II. Series.
HC108.C4C27 1997
338.6"042—dc21
                                                    97-35311

Printed on acid-free, 250-year-life paper
Manufactured in the United States of America

For SMCs

Contents

List of Tables ix
List of Figures xi
Preface xiii
Acknowledgments xvii

I. THE CENTRAL QUESTION 3
    Why Companies Locate Where They Do 3
        Traditional Location Theory 3
        Geography of Industry 6
    This Study: Branch Firms in the Chicago Suburbs 8
        Chicago, Illinois 9
    Outline of Following Chapters 11

II. PREVIOUS STUDIES OF COMPANY LOCATIONS 13
    Workers 16
    Material Inputs 26
    Energy 28
    Fiscal Influences --Taxes 28
    Site Attributes 30
    Market Factors 32
    Personal Factors 33
    Summary 35

III. DATA AND METHOD 39
    Why Both a Survey and a Model? 39
    Suburban Cities and Firms 41
        The Cities 41
        The Firms 41
    The Statistical Model and Municipal Database 46

	The Dependent Variables 48
	The Independent Variables 48
	The Survey 59
	Developing the Survey Instrument 59
	Survey Administration 59

IV. THE EVIDENCE: DETERMINANTS OF FIRM
    LOCATION 65
      What Does the Model Tell Us? 65
        Transportation Access 68
        City Characteristics 72
        Proximity to Other Businesses 72
        Tax Rate 73
        Labor Force 74
        Fit and Limitations of the Model 74
        Reduced Form Equation 77
        Evidence for Cities of 10,000 and Greater
        Population 77
      Evidence From the Survey 80
        Where Did the Firms Come From ? 80
        Reasons for Choosing the Suburbs 81
        Reasons for Choosing a Particular City 82
        A Special Look at Women Workers 83
      Comparing the Survey to the Database 86
        The Method 88
        The Variables 88
        Which Variables Capture Survey Answers?....... 90
        Conclusions 94

V. CONCLUDING REMARKS 103
      Typical Location Factors 103
      Women Workers and Firm Location 104
      Implications for Development and Labor 105
Appendix 1 107
Appendix 2 115
References 119
Index 125

List of Tables

1. Employment in the Chicago Metropolitan Area,
   1978-1990 10
2. Review of Previous Location Studies 15
3. Branch Firm by Industry 43
4. Descriptive Statistics For Independent Variables 51
5. Disposition of Surveys 60
6. Sample and Returns by Industry 61
7. City Variables: For Sampled and Responding Firms 63
8. Regression Coefficients - 203 Suburban Cities 67
9. Correlation Coefficients 69
10. Significant Studentized Residual Terms by
    Dependent Variable 76
11. Reduced Form Regression Coefficients - 203
    Suburban Cities 78
12. Regression Coefficients - Cities of 10,000
    and Greater 79
13. Companies Which Checked "Yes, Factor
    was Important" by Industry Type 81
14. Frequency of Survey Responses by Q8D
    (Female Labor was Important) 85
15. Frequency of Survey Responses by Women
    Workers Employed 87
16. Means and Standard Deviations for 85 Cities
    with Survey Returns 89
17. Means and Significance Levels for Difference
    of Means Tests on Selected City Variables 96
18. Municipalities Included in the Study 107

List of Figures

1. Number of Firms by Municipality 44
2. Branch Employment by Municipality 45

Preface

This book examines the role women workers who live in the suburbs play in drawing companies from central cities to suburban locations. A movement of jobs from cities to suburbs, which started during WWII and accelerated with the construction of the interstate highway system, has meant a substantial loss of jobs for central city residents, especially those restricted to living and working in inner-city neighborhoods because of transportation and housing barriers. This out-migration of economic activity has not only meant that fewer jobs are available to inner-city residents, but has also resulted in decreased tax revenues for central city services, a population shift from the central city to the suburbs as people follow jobs, and region-wide increased demands for highways and other infrastructure improvements to accommodate an increasingly decentralized population. The sprawl of population and jobs outside central cities thus has consequences for urban and suburban residents and governments.

Reasons for the movement from central cities to suburbs have focused on "bad" conditions in the cities and "good" conditions in the suburbs. Businesses are fleeing the inner city, it is said, because it is too congested, there is too much crime, central city taxes are too high, big-city bureaucracy is rampant, and buildings are crumbling and land is contaminated. In the suburbs firms can find plenty of relatively untouched land, good highways, a good quality of life, and a friendly city government.

However, one element which works to draw companies to the suburbs that is not discussed as much is the kind of workers that are available outside central cities. There is evidence that firms are drawn to the suburbs in order to tap a supply of white, middle-class women with good basic skills who are not the primary source of their family's income. Companies are moving to the suburbs in order to tap into a pool of workers whose presence in central cities has been shrinking in the post-war years—relatively well-educated, stable, non-minority women, primarily clerical workers, who prefer jobs close to home. Since these women tend to avoid long trips to and from work because of family responsibilities, companies must move to the suburbs rather than expect that the women will commute into the city.

These women have come to live in the suburbs for a variety of reasons. Some women live in households which moved to the suburbs in order to live in new cities that sprang up after WWII; cities that serve as residential "bedroom" communities for returning veterans who worked downtown. Office work has moved from cities to suburbs, in campus-like office developments along highway nodes, and their new locations attract nearby women looking to supplement the family's income.

Other women live in relatively far-flung suburbs which historically had a thriving manufacturing economy that was independent of their central city. As the Midwest and Northeast portions of the U.S. began to experience a loss of manufacturing jobs in the 1980s, these women have found themselves drawn into the labor market into jobs that are new to their towns. Replacing the watch factories, sweeper companies, and plastic molding operations that their fathers worked in, these women have found employment opportunities in the credit card customer service offices, inventory tracking agencies, and data entry companies which have recently moved in.

Do these women play a role in enticing businesses to the suburbs? What kinds of firms are looking for these women workers? What other factors besides women workers do companies take into account when deciding where to locate their businesses? Previous studies of company locations, as mentioned, have shown how highway access, available land, city tax rates, zoning, and etc., are all other factors that businesses consider when deciding where to go. Are these factors primary or is there evidence that, besides these considerations, companies think about an available labor pool made up of women workers when deciding to choose a location?

This book addresses these questions by looking at companies in suburban cities in the Chicago metropolitan area. I come at these questions using two techniques: a survey of business, which can give us qualitative, hands-on information; and a mathematical model, which reveals relationships between company locations and city characteristics that the survey can't reveal. This study is one of only a very few that use both methods to look at business locations. The mathematical model is a standard regression equation. The output from the equation is presented, and the discussion tries to be non-technical for those readers who may not be familiar with such statistical methods.

My study is of branch firms in particular--that is, companies with more than one office or factory location, and one of their locations (branches) is in the Chicago suburbs. The reason for looking at branch plants is that "single-site" firms, firms with only one office, tend to be found situated in cities in a somewhat random fashion. The choice of a site for a branch firm, however, is usually fairly rigorous, where company personel take many factors into consideration before choosing a place to locate. So, in terms of investigating factors important to company locations, as this book does, it makes more sense to look at branch firms than at single-site firms who are not likely to have taken such factors into account.

This study focuses solely on manufacturing and business services companies. Construction, agriculture, government and consumer services are not treated. Construction is left out because it is not an economic activity that is "located in space" per se. There may be one or two or many offices, but the work does not take place in that office— it takes places on hundreds of construction sites across the city. Agriculture, obviously, has no offices, although there may be some services that serve farmers from offices nearby. The location of government offices and consumer services (such as barber shops, record stores, supermarkets, and other activities that serve the people who live in a city) is dictated almost solely by the size and incomes of city residents.

The implication of answers to the question of women workers are many. Economic development officials in central cities need to know what is special about their "economic competitors" in the suburbs that surround them. What are they up against when trying to persuade companies to choose a downtown location? Is it that the city lacks the kinds of workers for which businesses are looking? Perhaps then job training for central city residents, or education to firms about the kinds of workers that may be found in the city. Or are the considerations that tip the scale in favor of the suburbs a host of other traditional factors, such as land costs and congestion? Can city officials address any of these?

The economic fortunes of suburban cities are also affected by the answers to these questions. If women workers are important to particular kinds of firms, then how can cities without these women compete? What happens as this labor force moves further out, away from suburbs near downtown to more remote locations? In addition, what about those suburban cities that were historically independent, economically, from the central city but now found themselves drawn into the larger regional economy through population shifts and transportation improvements? For these cities, does their economic success, their ability to move from an industrial, manufacturing-based economy to a service-oriented economy, depend on the presence of these women workers? If so, then residential development, inasmuch as it attracts workers who then attract firms, is important to their continued economic health. And, by realizing the economic potential posed by the presence of these women workers, development officials can perhaps broaden their development strategies and consciously recruit firms for whom these workers are appropriate labor.

However, there are also broader career implications for women who work in these suburban branch plants. As these women progress up the internal promotion ladder as much as they are able and willing, at some point moving from the suburban branch operation to a headquarters or another branch firm might mean a longer commute, or perhaps a move. To the extent that they are the family's second source of income, and have family responsibilities that are primary, they may forgo that next promotion that requires them to spend more time on the road.

This study is one of only a handful of business location studies done in the 1990s and the first to use traditional methods (a survey and a model) to investigate the role of women workers. The question of business location decisions was more researched in the 1980s, when a major concern for scholars was the loss of manufacturing jobs in the Northeast and Midwest regions of the U.S. The concern then was to identify why companies seemed to be so mobile, to ascertain those factors that induced firms to leave the "snowbelt" and relocate to the south and west. There was also an interest then in accounting for the effect of taxes on development—were high tax rates driving out companies?—and a slate of studies in the 1980s looked specifically at the effect of taxes. This book is also the first company location study which systematically looks at the importance of women workers while also taking into account traditional factors that have influenced company locations.

Acknowledgments

Of course any one piece of scholarship, although authored by one or a few, is in reality the work of many along the way. This book would not have been possible without the continued support of Anne Shlay, now at Temple University, who first awakened my interest in social science research. Wim Wiewel and Joseph Persky, both of the University of Illinois at Chicago, were available to discuss urban decentralization. The Federal Reserve Bank of Chicago and the University of Illinois at Chicago Center for Urban Economic Development provided mail services, data and research assistant support, espcially Kathy Kolnick at UIC, and David Ruder and Robert Mcnamara at the Chicago Fed. Jim Horan, my research assistant at the University of Wisconsin-Milwaukee deserves a special mention for painstaking attention to detail in research and is also responsible for the book's being correct in spelling, grammar, and formatting. Faculty at the University of Wisconsin-Milwaukee provided crucial scholarly insights. Thanks also must go to women who throughout the years have worked for the right of women everywhere to have financial and emotional independence.

The Availability of
Women Workers

I
The Central Question

The explanations traditionally given by urban economists for the movement of jobs from cities to suburbs have focused on conditions that affect companies' bottom line and so "push" firms from the central city, such as high crime rates; outmoded streets, bridges and sewers; environmentally contaminated industrial sites; traffic congestion; and high tax rates. Fewer studies have considered elements that may "pull" firms to the suburbs; that is, looked at favorable conditions that entice firms to suburban sites. What this book does is to look at the importance of women workers in drawing firms to the suburbs. Recent work by Nelson (1986) and Garreau (Garreau 1991, 112) suggest that women draw firms to the suburbs in order to tap a supply of white, middle-class women with good basic skills who are not the primary source of their family's income.

WHY COMPANIES LOCATE WHERE THEY DO

Other factors besides labor have historically been the central topic of investigation into what influences a company to choose a particular location. How and why labor force characteristics influence what sites companies choose are questions that have only recently become of interest to researchers, but this interest has grown out of the work that came before. Let us look at the development of what is called "location theory" and how this body of literature has come to be interested in workers and the role they play.

Traditional Location Theory
Early research which was concerned with identifying factors that affect companies' decisions to choose one or another site (called "industrial

location theory") was dominated by economists and focused mainly on manufacturing firms and suggested that firms chose their sites primarily to minimize the costs of transporting inputs such as labor and raw materials to the company, and then shipping finished products out of the company (Weber 1929). It was assumed that inputs were only available from certain places, and that the product was shipped to a market where it could be sold for a fixed price (that is, a price not set by the company, but set by the workings of the marketplace where there are several sellers). Optimal firm location was then considered to be that point at which the cost of transporting inputs from the field to the factory and transporting finished products to market was at its lowest. Given that several locations will most likely fit this criteria, a company would then take into consideration "agglomeration economies:" the types of other businesses nearby, the relative amount of other economic activity, and the general level of development at the different sites. For example, having found several least-transportation-cost sites, the company might situate itself near other compatible companies (for example, a tomato-canning factory might build on a site near a juice-making factory, with the idea that people looking for jobs at the juice-making factory might also then also apply at their tomato-canning factory and so have compatible skills; or, a button factory might locate near garment manufacturers, because they have to work closely with other companies in the fashion industry). Or, they may decide to chose a location where the general level of economic activity is high, to take advantage of services that tend to crop up near busy locations, such as printing services, banks, delivery messengers, etc.

Two other urban economists, Greenhut (1956) and Losch (1954), added to this theory by suggesting that it was not only transportation costs that might be different at different locations, but also that prices of the finished products would be higher or lower at different places depending on competition from other firms. The question of location for the firm is thus not just keeping transportation costs low, but also getting the highest price at the market as possible. The best location will vary for businesses in different industries, because as input requirements and markets vary by industry. These discoveries by Greenhut and Losch paved the way for location theorists to become more than mere straightforward transportation cost estimators. Instead, a host of factors had to be explored. Thus those researchers concerned with company location and the economic

The Central Question

development of places now started to work "on the ground," asking firms directly what was important to their decisions to chose one or another location, and incorporating a much more rich set of factors in their economic models.

Since that time, location theory has been dominated by the groundwork laid in research by Roger Schmenner (1975, 1978, 1980, 1982). His work encompasses a broad range of industries, with in-depth company interviews as well as statistical models. One of Schmenner's major contributions to the field which is relevant to the consideration of labor as a factor in employers' site choices is the conclusion that location decisions are best thought of as occurring in stages, where the geographic area under consideration narrows at each stage. Based on his insight, it is now generally conceived that a business selects a location in two geographic stages. First a broad region or state is chosen, then the particular city and site (McMillan 1965; Schmenner, Huber and Cook 1987). In this argument, the importance of any particular location factor varies between stages, according to how the factor varies across geographic units and its relative effect on the cost of production or access to markets. For example, the presence or absence of "right-to-work" laws is thought to affect the choice of a particular state or group of states, because states, not cities, enact such laws. In a similar manner, tax rates influence the choice of a municipality, not a region, since regional differences in such things as energy costs and labor will outweigh any differences in state tax rates (Cornia, Testa, and Stocker 1978, 2).

Most of the work which investigates how attributes of the labor supply, such as availability and cost, influences firms' site choices examines the importance of workers to the *first* stage of the decision. The main focus has been on wage rates paid to workers, and the biggest differences are found among large geographic areas, such as states or counties. Little work has been done which tests how important labor force factors may be when measured against other factors that companies consider when making the second-stage decision, i.e., the decision to choose a particular city and site.

Because the research into city-level site choices has been dominated by those interested in public finance issues, studies whose interest is primarily in the role of fiscal factors, especially property tax rates, are almost too numerous to name (see Bartik 1991, and the discussion in the next chapter, for a review). Labor force factors are included as "control" variables or minor variables of interest in a few studies and their effect on location duly noted (Erickson and Wasylenko 1980, McGuire 1985, Wasylenko 1980), but are not the primary interest of the research. This is unfortunate, especially since some studies in this "traditional" vein have found that labor factors are more important than fiscal factors in predicting the location of businesses among cities (Schmenner 1975, Erickson and Wasylenko 1980).

The Geography of Industry

Given the reluctance of traditional location theory to fully explore the role of workers in determining business location choices, it has been left to geographers researching industrial patterns to suggest the importance of labor. This began in the early 1970s when Doreen Massey built on the idea in location theory that there was a host of factors affecting employer site choices, but took traditional industrial location economists to task for ignoring the fact that location choices are geographically specific, that is, they happen in a particular place, and thus affect and are affected by the people and social groups who live in that place (Massey 1973). The site choices of firms, by extension, affect the economic development of places and so affect the economic fortunes of people who live there. Those following Massey have focused on the effects changes in technology, transportation and information flows have had on the relation between capital and labor in regions and communities and how communities have fared when company investments have declined (Massey 1978, 1984; Storper and Walker 1983; Scott 1988; Scott and Soja, 1996).

In this perspective, the development of places (neighborhoods, cities and regions) is closely tied to the distinctive characteristics of workers who live there. Since the characteristics of labor differ across space (high-skilled, low-skilled, etc.), and so attract different kinds of industries, development can be characterized as a *spatial division of labor* (Storper and Walker 1983). Different kinds of industries, and businesses, will locate in different places in order to take advantage of the variability in workers skills, because workers are not very mobile. One can have other inputs to the production process transported from far-flung places (lumber, silicon chips, paper, etc. can all be shipped in), but workers, as people with homes and children, are rooted in particular communities. Therefore, companies must locate where the workers with the desired skills live, and by their location choices they affect the level of economic development and opportunities available to workers. Then, places become the center for one or another kind of industry.

The Central Question

For example, some larger regions become the center for major industries, such as Silicon Valley in California, or Detroit, the Motor City. In larger cities, different neighborhoods may come to specialize in various products, such as the old meatpacking industry in Chicago, clustered on the near southwest side in neighborhoods dominated by Polish and Irish immigrants. Companies' knowledge of the way in which labor characteristics are different across space has been revealed by Hanson and Pratt in firm interviews conducted in Worcester, Massachusetts (Hanson and Pratt 1992, 1995). Their research demonstrates that businesses make intra-metropolitan, (sub-city) location decisions based on a finely-tuned knowledge of the geography of the labor market. Labor market sub-groups, or segments, based not just on specific skills, but also on other attributes that employers thought would be associated with appropriate labor, such as gender and ethnicity, live in different places, that is, are "geographically specific." Hanson and Pratt found that firms choose locations to tap these segments. For example, in the company interviews, personnel managers were found to report things such as "we were looking for Eastern European immigrants with metalworking skills" (Hanson and Pratt 1992, 379).

Kirsten Nelson documented this phenomenon for the San Francisco-Oakland SMSA during the early to mid 1980s (Nelson 1986). She studied one labor market segment in particular: middle-class, white, second-earner women in the suburbs who seek employment opportunities which are characterized by a short work-trip distance and low responsibility. Nelson specifically looked at the extent to which the movement of back office development (such as credit card processing and other "behind the scenes" large-batch, routine office work) from the central city to the suburbs could be attributed to the presence in the suburbs of these women. What she found is that such kinds of employers were very conscious about having chosen a suburban location in order to be near these women. A host of these companies had established company policies, such as flexible work schedules and day care centers, specifically in order to attract these women workers. These companies knew that they had to move to the suburbs in order to find these women, that because of family responsibilities these women were unlikely to commute to downtown or more central areas.

THIS STUDY: BRANCH FIRMS IN THE CHICAGO SUBURBS

Since Nelson's work in 1986, there has been continued interest in examining the special situation of suburban women workers. Several researchers continue to document the time and distance constraints on women's commute to work outside central cities on which Nelson's work is partially based (Johnston-Anumonwo 1997, MacDonald and Peters 1994). Other writers have focused on how the geography of jobs affects the special occupational niches that women workers tend to occupy (England 1993, Hanson and Pratt 1991). However, no further study has been done of the special role than women in the suburbs fill in enticing employers to the suburbs. Identifying the forces at work encouraging suburban sprawl seems especially important because of the effects this sprawl has on job availability for central city workers, and other concomitant regional problems, such as suburban gridlock, infrastructure demands, and inner-city disinvestment (Massey and Denton 1993; Persky, Sclar and Wiewel 1991). Nelson's work suggests that it is not only, and perhaps not primarily, transportation and other cost factors shifting development to the suburbs, but that it is access to a particular kind of labor force. If the proximity to white, middle-class, women workers is important to employers, then efforts to revitalize the inner-city must recognize this competition. For example, "reverse commuting" strategies, which attempt to link central-city residents to jobs in the suburbs, may encounter barriers because suburban employers are not looking for the types of labor found in central cities. In addition, economic development programs aimed at reducing the cost of doing business for firms in central cities, such as tax breaks for capital investment, may not have the effects intended, because it may be that companies are avoiding central city sites for labor, not cost, reasons.

The importance to firms of women workers is also important for suburban cities on the metropolitan periphery which have traditionally relied upon a "male" manufacturing base for economic viability. Such cities were historically far enough away from their nearest central city so that commuting to this downtown location before the federal highway system was in place was not likely. Consequently, these places developed an economic base relatively independent from the central city. To the extent that such peripheral cities have lost manufacturing jobs along with the rest of the northeast and midwest, to a large extent their economic well-being may now depend on whether they have managed to capture some of the economic activity moving out of older urban centers. Are women important in this process?

It seems appropriate to specifically consider the location of branch activity rather than single site firms for several reasons. First, because Schmenner's research has illustrated how branch establishments (subsidiaries or units of larger corporations), as opposed to single-site firms (firms with only one physical location), undergo a rigorous location decision making process where a list of priorities is developed and sites evaluated against such a list (Schmenner 1982, 47). Single-site firms are more likely to be situated due to chance, so that the distribution of labor or other site characteristics may not bear a relation to an observed pattern of firm location For example, many firm owners start up a firm near their own home for the first few years, to test whether the firm will be viable, then later make a more reasoned, "rational" decision about location, taking several factors into account (more on branches vs. single-site locations appears in the next chapter). Secondly, Nelson's work suggests that women workers are especially important to the location choices of back office operations, which by definition are branch establishments. In particular it is entry-level, or lower-end "pink-collar" clerical jobs for which firms are looking to tap women workers, and these occupations are more likely to be found in branch operations.

Chicago, Illinois

The analysis presented here focuses on the Chicago, Illinois metropolitan area, which consists of Cook, DuPage, Kane, Lake, McHenry and Will counties in northeastern Illinois. The metropolitan area is dominated by the city of Chicago itself, with a 1990 population of just under 3 million. The total metropolitan population is just over 7 million.

The Chicago area is not unlike others in the northeast and midwest in that it has suffered a net loss of manufacturing employment in the 1980s and experienced a dispersion of employment from the central city to the suburbs during that time (table 1). The metropolitan area can be classified into three parts: the city of Chicago itself; inner-ring Cook county suburbs, many with a decidedly industrial flavor; and outer-ring suburban cities which include

Table 1
Employment in the Chicago Metropolitan Area, 1978-1990 (Thousands)

	1978		1990		% Change	
	Total	Mfg.	Total	Mfg.	Total	Mfg.
Total 6 counties	2,523.9	789.5	3,059.5	653.4	21.2	-17.2
Chicago city	1,205.7	352.1	1,201.1	216.2	-.4	-38.6
Inner-ring suburbs[a]	595.1	211.6	665.8	149.6	11.9	-29.3
Outer-ring suburbs[b]	723.1	225.8	1,192.6	287.6	64.9	27.4
Outer belt cities	121.8	43.2	129.6	28.3	6.4	-34.5

Source: Illinois Department of Employment Security, 1979, 1991.
Note: 1990 was the latest year chosen because changes in reporting methods render post-1990 data not comparable to earlier years.

[a] Inner-ring suburbs include all Cook county suburban areas as defined in *Where Workers Work*, except Northwest Suburban (roughly defined as the portion of Cook county which lies above DuPage county).

[b] Outer-ring suburbs include the five suburban counties plus the Cook County Northwest Suburban area described in the previous footnote. Outer-ring belt cities include Elgin, Aurora, Joliet, and Waukegan. These cities are a subset of "outer ring suburbs."

post-WWII suburban "bedroom" communities, older peripheral industrial towns, and rural agricultural centers. An examination of employment in these rings, can tells us how development has moved out from the central city. The central city portion of total metropolitan area employment dropped from 48% in 1978 to 39% in 1990. Manufacturing jobs dispersed at an even greater rate: Chicago's portion of such jobs slipped from 45% to 33%.

Inner-ring industrial towns include such cities as Cicero, Berwyn and Franklin Park. Many residents were drawn to the area to work at the Hawthorn Works of Western Electric in Cicero, which opened in 1903 and in 1950 employed 13,000 people (McDonald 1984). However, the inner-ring area experienced a 29% decline in manufacturing employment, and has seen its share of metropolitan manufacturing employment slip from 27% to 23%. Suburban minority populations are clustered in the south portion of the Cook county suburbs, in cities such as Harvey, Dixmoor, and Hazel Crest.

The outer-ring suburbs experienced the bulk of metropolitan employment growth in both total and manufacturing employment. Their

The Central Question

share of metropolitan manufacturing employment grew from 29% to 44%. It was the only sub-metropolitan area to experience overall manufacturing growth. Communities such as Schaumburg, Naperville, Arlington Heights, and Elmhurst established primarily as residential communities in the years after WWII, each experienced employment growth from 1978 to 1990 of over 150% (Illinois Department of Employment Security 1979, 1991).

The growth of peripheral industrial towns in this outer ring was encouraged by transportation improvements in freight during the late 1800s and early 1900s. The development of the railroad beltways outside the city spurred residential and business decentralization. In particular, an outer railway belt line was completed in 1887 which circles Chicago and intersects trunk lines from Chicago at a distance of about 25 to 40 miles from the Loop. The line connects Porter, Indiana to Joliet, Aurora, Elgin, with a terminus in Waukegan. Cities along this periphery are those referred to above--cities which early on developed an economic base independent from Chicago. Early businesses to choose sites along this route were the Inland Steel mill in Chicago Heights (25 miles south of the Loop), Caterpillar (industrial and heavy machinery manufacturing) in Aurora (37 miles southwest), and the Elgin Watch factory in Elgin (39 miles west). Unlike the outer-ring area in general, these peripheral industrial towns have experienced much the same employment losses as Chicago: stagnant total employment, and manufacturing losses of over 30%.

Finally, this outer-ring is still home to agricultural production. The outermost portions of the Kane, McHenry, and Will counties are dotted by small towns which serve primarily as shopping and banking places for outlying farm residents: Burlington and Hampshire in Kane County, Huntley and Hebron in McHenry County.

OUTLINE OF FOLLOWING CHAPTERS

The next chapter looks at previous location studies, highlighting findings regarding factors influencing company site choices, with particular emphasis on investigations that have considered the role of labor force characteristics. As will be demonstrated, studies which consider the influence of worker traits in the sub-metropolitan siting of firms are relatively rare. Most studies that look at labor do so from a metropolitan or regional standpoint. Chapter three then outlines the methods by which the study presented in this book went about examining the location decisions of suburban branch establishments in the Chicago area. Both a survey of firms as well as a statistical model were used. The findings regarding the relative importance of women workers, as well as other factors such as transportation accessibility, land costs, etc., is then discussed in Chapter four. Chapter five is a concluding look at the work.

II
Previous Studies of Company Locations

The question, "what factors influence company location decisions?" has been addressed by a wealth of previous studies, some of which were touched on briefly in the previous chapter. This book presents research primarily concerned with the role played by women workers in drawing firms to the suburbs, but other studies have considered transportation costs and accessibility, tax rates, "quality of life" issues, and other considerations taken into account by company executives when choosing a site for their firm. This chapter takes a look at the most influential of these other studies, in order to put this book in historical perspective; to introduce the techniques by which this question has been explored by other work--techniques also used in this research; and to examine what has already been discovered regarding the importance of workers, so that we might know what this study adds to existing knowledge. Studies by both industrial location economists and industrial geographers, discussed in the previous chapter, are presented.

Note that this book is primarily concerned with examining the reasons why individual companies choose one or another site on which to place themselves. This includes companies that are moving from another location as well as companies just starting out. But new locations by companies are only one component of what affects the total level of employment in an area over time. *Net* employment change in a city is a result not only of new firms starting up ("firm births") or moving to the area ("firm relocations"), but also from other firms leaving or closing ("deaths"), and existing firms either adding new workers ("expansions") or laying off workers ("contractions"). Some of the same factors that influence company decisions about choosing a site may also affect company decisions to leave, or contract, or expand, and have spawned other schools of research, but here, only studies of firm relocations are reviewed.

The discussion is organized around specific variables that businesses consider: production cost factors (labor and other material inputs, fiscal considerations such as taxes, and site attributes); market factors (consumer characteristics and agglomeration economies); and personal considerations. A last summary section draws conclusions and compares the variables (i.e., does the evidence suggest one or another variable is more or less important than others?).

A matrix of the major location studies reviewed here is presented in table 2. (Two studies are referred to briefly in pages to follow but are not studies of firm location per se, so are not included in table 2 [Fox 1981 and McHone 1986]). Three themes run through the discussion. First is the stage of the location decision. The introductory chapter mentioned that Schmenner (1982) demonstrated how firm location decisions are made at several geographic levels. First a general region, area, or state is chosen, then the particular city and site. These decisions are referred to as "first stage" and "second stage" choices. The factors that companies take into account are different at different stages, depending on whether inter-state (stage one) or inter-municipality (stage two) location decisions are being investigated.

The second theme concerns the type of business under investigation: branch plants or single-site firms. It has been demonstrated that decisions to locate branch plants are usually made in a more systematic fashion than is the case for single site firms. The locating of a single site firm tends to be influenced more by historical accident and personal considerations--near the owner's home or workplace, for example. Therefore the factors that are of importance will vary depending upon the type of firm being studied. Some analyses examine both branches and single-site firms in the same study; however, of these, Kieschnick (discussed below) was the only one to report separate analysis for the two groups. For the others, therefore, it is not possible to separate factors important to each type of firm. However, other studies only looked at one of the company types; for example, Carlton reported on single-site firms in 1979 and branches in 1983; likewise Schmenner focused on different firm types in different studies.

The final theme pertains to the methodology employed. Two major techniques have been employed in location research--surveys and statistical models. Surveys consist of direct information gathered from key informants at businesses who were involved with or have knowledge about how the site was chosen. Surveys can take the form of short questionnaires, either mailed

Table 2
Dimensions of Reviewed Firm Location Studies

Author (Date)	Method		Stage			Firm Type		Sample/dependent variable
	Survey	Model	State	Local		Single	Branch	
Mueller & Morgan (62)	X			X		X	X	Michigan manufacturing firms
McMillan (65)	X			X		X	X	National sample manufacturing firms
Moses & Williamson (67)		X						Chicago mfg relocations/area
Stafford (74)	X		X			X	X	Manufacturing firms in southeast Ohio
Schmenner (75)		X		X		X	X	Movers, densities, various large cities
Fortune, Inc. (77)	X		X					Sample of 1,000 large manufacturers
Schmenner (78)	X		X			X	X	Manufacturers in Cincinnati and New England
Carlton (79)		X	X			X	X	National sample manufacturing firms
Schmenner (80)	X		X					Sample Fortune 500 companies
Erickson & Wasylenko (80)		X		X		X	X	Movers from Milwaukee to suburban location
Wasylenko (80)		X		X		X	X	Movers from Milwaukee to suburban location
Kieschnick (81)	X		X			X	X	*Manufacturing firms w/capital investments
Epping (82)	X		X			X	X	Arkansas manufacturing firms
Charney (83)		X		X		X		Detroit, Michigan movers
Carlton (83)		X	X			X	X	National sample manufacturing firms
Nelson (84)	X		X				X	Back offices in San Francisco
Bartik (85)		X		X			X	Sample Fortune 500 companies
McGuire (85)		X	X			X	X	Minneapolis-St. Paul MN building permits
Schmenner, Huber & Cook (87)		X	X				X	Sample Fortune 500 companies
Lopez & Henderson (89)	X			X				Northeast food processors
Johnson (91)	X			X			X	Southern rural manufacturing
Hanson & Pratt (91)	X			X		X	X	Mfg. producers services in Worchester, Mass.
Kriesel & McNamara (91)		X		X		X	X	GA counties # new plants

15

to the company or completed in-person by the researcher, or can consist of longer, in-depth, personal interviews. Statistical models are mathematical estimates of the relationship between the number of businesses, or level of employment in those businesses in particular places, to a set of factors that the investigator thinks influences businesses site choices. These factors need to be easily "countable" or "quantifiable" so that the math can be performed. For example, "distance to central city" and "municipal tax rate" are quantifiable variables.

Each method has advantages as well as drawbacks. Surveys enable the researcher to do a relatively fine-grained analysis of the location decision process, in that the researcher is able to ask about factors not easily counted (e.g., quality of life considerations such as "how good are the nearby schools?") or factors that differ among industrial sectors (e.g., access to specific inputs, because different kinds of businesses require different kinds of inputs).

On the other hand, statistical models provide a more precise measure of the effect of particular variables on the location process (e.g., for every one percent increase in the tax rate 10 few companies will choose your city). Statistical models also are not susceptible to questions of historical memory as are surveys, where the analyst must rely on an individual's recollection.

WORKERS

One problem in weighing the evidence for and against the importance of workers to the location decision of firms is that studies of business location decisions differ, sometimes markedly, in terms of the particular worker characteristics deemed important enough to study and then how the characteristic is measured. Perhaps the availability of workers is the concern. How does one measure it? Unemployment rate? Workers employed? Working age population? A general supply of labor, or a particular kind of skilled or unskilled worker? Or perhaps unionization is suspected to influence industry location. But do we mean the number of workers that belong to unions? Or are we more concerned about days of work lost to strikes? Or are companies just looking for states with "right-to-work" laws? Compounding the differences is the methodology employed. As discussed above, survey or interview answers, by nature, are subjective, while econometric studies are forced to choose a measure that can capture the characteristic in a "number." For example, while surveys may ask company managers general questions about the importance of workers, such as "a good labor climate" or "labor advantages," statistical or econometric models must include a variable that can be quantified, such as "percent of workers belonging to a union," or "wages paid per worker," etc. Anyone trying to compare the findings from surveys to finding from statistical models is confronted with the need to decide whether the two works are really investigating the same variable. Such complications are not nearly so extreme for most other factors. That is, aspects such as "distance to the central business district" or "access to highways" are more or less easily measured and understood.

Part of the reason for the inexact treatment of worker characteristics is the fact that few studies in the industrial location tradition were designed specifically to investigate the importance of workers. Although virtually all published studies of business location decisions include some labor force measure(s), in surveys these measures are included as one factor among several investigated, and in statistical models most often only as "control variables" in models whose primary concern is the importance of other variables (usually taxes). Under these conditions, there is little reason to rigorously define what is meant by various measures of "labor force characteristics." Exceptions include studies in the industrial geography literature (discussed below) which were undertaken specifically to investigate labor force factors and have more rigorously probed the labor force question and report labor force information in more detail. But these studies consist mainly of firm interviews focused on worker characteristics and so cannot say much about the *relative* importance of labor force factors compared to other variables.

In general, though, labor force factors reported in the literature come under one of four broad headings: the cost of labor, such as wages, benefit levels, and unemployment insurance rates; the general availability of workers; unionization; and labor productivity (output per worker). While surveys have attempted to gauge the importance of all four kinds of factors, statistical models have not included productivity variables, probably because productivity is difficult to measure and so the kind of data needed for statistical models is hard to come by. It is also sometimes unclear what is meant by "labor productivity" in survey questions; it is likely that in many instances it could be a proxy for "unionization" or "work ethic." With this said, five general points can be summarized from the studies in table 2.

First is the finding that workers, generally, are at least as important as most other considerations for both first and second stage choices; however; the labor attributes for which firms are looking differ between stages one and two. At the first stage, labor considerations vie for importance with two other factors that differ at the state or regional level (proximity to markets, proximity to customers). At the second stage, worker characteristics are again important along with a set of other factors that varies among municipalities or smaller places, such as transportation access, land costs, and access to specific sub-regional markets.

Yet, as one might suspect, "worker characteristics" encompass a range of attributes, some of which will vary by state/region (first stage) and others of which will vary by smaller levels of geography (second stage), so that different labor factors come into play at the state level than at the local level. There seem to be factors which vary among regions and states but not within a state, so that firms tend to take these particular labor variables into consideration when making the first cut and focus on others when selecting the city and site. Specifically, wage rates and unionization (and, for surveys "labor productivity") are distributed at the state and regional level (although there is some evidence for a wage gradient as one moves further from a central city), while the general availability of workers, and of appropriately-skilled labor specifically, and other demographic attributes (e.g., race and gender) vary among cities. Businesses thus tend to take these consider wage rates and unionization when making first-stage decisions, and to consider labor availability at the second stage.

For example, in surveys considering first-stage choices, "labor costs" or wages were ranked first by Mueller and Morgan (1962), second by Schmenner (1978), first for branches by Kieschnick (1981), fifth for Schmenner (1980), and first by Johnson (1991). "Labor productivity" was mentioned as among the top three factors affecting state location choices in surveys reported by Stafford (1974) and Fortune, Inc. (1977), and fourth for Johnson (1991). For statistical models, measures of labor cost in the form of wages are significant for Carlton (1979, which includes both branches and single-site firms), and Bartik (1985). (Measures of labor cost in terms of benefits and unemployment insurance levels turn out not to be significant in these models; Neither Schmenner, Huber and Cook nor Bartik find effects from benefit and unemployment insurance levels.) Both Bartik, and Schmenner, Huber and Cook find measures of unionization significant for state-level decisions. In addition, surveys that investigate both stages of the location process by the same set of firms find this first-stage/second-stage split to be the case. Administrators of firms in southeastern Ohio were interviewed by Stafford (1974). Labor productivity and wages rank second and fourth, respectively, in the factors they consider when first choosing a multi-state area; labor availability is ranked ninth. However, when asked what factors they looked for when choosing a particular community, labor availability jumped up to fourth, and labor rates declined to eighth. Schmenner's influential 1980 study looks at 410 *Fortune 500* firms in several manufacturing industries, including apparel, shoes, electronic equipment, defense contractors, and chemicals. "Favorable labor climate" (Schmenner defines this as unionization) is deemed crucial by 76% of firms considering region/state constraints, but by only 1% of those same firms when choosing a particular site. Finally, Johnson surveys 340 branch plants in the South. "Respondents ranked highly the need for low-cost labor at both the regional and the local levels; and at the local level considerable importance was attached to proximity to an abundance of workers who could be employed as assemblers and fabricators . . ." (Johnson 1991, 405).

It is also the case that studies which consider the state choice find wages and unionization more of a concern than labor attributes, while research on city locations tends to find the reverse. For example, Mueller and Morgan (1962) ask 239 manufacturing firms "why did you choose Michigan?" Firms rank labor costs first, while the availability of labor rank third behind proximity to markets. In the survey done on state decisions by Fortune (1977), respondents rate productivity of workers first, while the availability of unskilled and skilled workers rank tenth and eleventh. Bartik (1985) uses Schmenner's data to model state branch plant locations, and includes measures of labor costs (unionization and average wage) as well as labor attributes (median education). Unionization and wage variables are significant, while the median education level is not. Specifically, he estimates that a 10% increase in a state's unionization rate is associated with a 30-40% decline in the number of new branch plants. Schmenner, Huber and Cook (1987) find similar effects. They use data gathered from Schmenner's *Fortune 500* survey as well as a set of state descriptor variables to investigate the decision to locate new branch manufacturing facilities. A state's "right-to-work" status and "weeks lost to work stoppages" are significant; education variables are not.

Conversely, McMillan (1965), reports on a McGraw-Hill survey of about 2,000 firms which asked about the reasons for choosing a particular site. "Availability of labor skills" is mentioned by 48% of respondents, while labor rates rank lower (33% of respondents). The unemployment rate (what they termed "a proxy for labor availability") and race are significant predictors of plant locations (a positive and negative relation, respectively). In the industrial geography literature, Hanson and Pratt (1992) report on personal interviews conducted with both employers and employees in four areas in the Worcester, Massachusetts metropolitan area. They asked firms to list the kinds of labor regularly needed (skilled vs. unskilled, inexpensive vs. costly), and conclude that answers to this question differed in terms of the community where the firm was located. Firms in one particular area indicated they sought production workers, while companies in other areas claimed they needed engineers and other professionals. Overall, firms in two of the three communities ranked labor availability ahead of wage rates.

Statistical models also consistently report on the significance of labor force availability at the local level (in fact, statistical models are the method most often employed in investigating the municipal location decision, because the writing on this question has been dominated by researchers in the public finance tradition). Schmenner (1978) includes firm relocations along with establishment and employment densities as dependent variables in his study of Cincinnati, Cleveland, Kansas City, and Minneapolis-St. Paul in the late 1960s. While population density (which he interprets as a labor supply measure) is significant in predicting all three dependent variables, wage variables were not nearly as consistent. Erickson and Wasylenko (1980) and Wasylenko (1980) examine firms relocating from Milwaukee to any one of 56 suburbs between 1964 and 1974. A variable that measures current labor force participation by industry within commuting distance is important in explaining the choice of suburb for firms in all seven industry sectors. McGuire (1985) includes a significant measure of labor force availability within the surrounding county to predict new industrial building permits in the Minneapolis-St. Paul SMSA. This is the percentage of the total SMSA labor force that was located in the county of interest. Kriesel and McNamara (1991) model second-stage decisions (in this case, inter-county choices in Georgia). While "average weekly manufacturing wage" is not significant, a measure of labor availability (unemployment rate), *is*.

The second point regarding workers is here suggested by the review of municipal-level studies just presented. One must be careful in specifying and attempting to measure the effect a local supply of workers might have on employer locations, because the size of a workforce is closely related to the sheer physical size of a city and so to the presence of what are termed "agglomeration economies:" the types of other businesses nearby which might supply materials or serve as customers, and populations which may offer labor or serve as customers. In this case one may conclude that it is the presence of workers, as city residents, when really the factor drawing businesses to the city is the presence of numerous other kinds of activities also being supported. Population-based measures (such as "number of workers" or merely "population") that are hypothesized as measuring labor accessibility could simply be a proxy for the physical size of the city. When the dependent variable is a count of firms or some other quantity measure (building permits to McGuire, number of new plant announcements to Kriesel and McNamara, etc.) one would expect the quantity to be larger where the city or county was larger, and to be related to population merely because of size, not because population is the same as labor force availability. One would need land area measures to better isolate the difference between size and labor availability. Likewise, general labor force availability measures (i.e., "employment density" or "number of manufacturing workers) could be a proxy for the presence of other potential suppliers and buyers, and not labor force availability per se.

A good model must take all three factors (land area, agglomeration economies and labor force availability) into account in order to isolate the effects of labor force availability. (This is less important for state-level choices, where firms are considering other factors and assuming that an appropriate labor force is available in *some* community within the state). Published work generally has included one or two but not all three. For example, Charney (1983) investigates zip codes in the three county Detroit area and includes "employment density" (employment/land area) as an independent variable. She also defines her dependent variable as the number of locating firms divided by land area. Because the measures implicitly control for land area, they distinguish agglomeration economies or the presence of a trained work force from the effects of sheer size. The employment density variable is significant in predicting the location of firms across size classes. Yet "employment density" does not itself distinguish industrial activity from labor force availability (that is, is it the firms or is it the workers?). McGuire includes population density as well as labor force proportions, but neglects to control for agglomeration effects and thus cannot distinguish the two. She notes this: ". . . this variable [percent of labor force in county] may be a proxy for agglomeration economies and thus a positive coefficient is consistent with this interpretation also" (McGuire 1985, 230). Likewise, the "labor force participation within commuting distance" variable used by the Erickson and Wasylenko and Wasylenko studies also doesn't distinguish labor force availability from the general level of industrial activity. Kriesel and McNamara's study avoids this problem somewhat by including an insignificant variable "number of manufacturing workers" along with the significant "unemployment rate" measure referred to above, but suffers in that it does not include a "size of county" measure (whether land area or population). Schmenner's 1975 study manages to avoid the problem by including both population (which he interprets as labor force availability) and establishment densities as independent variables. His dependent variables are also measured as densities, so that there is no need to control for land area.

The third area of discussion concerns the contention that branch plants in general are sited through a more methodical, "rational," process than is true for single-site firms. Headquarters looking to locate branch plants employ a deliberate siting strategy, while single-site employers often find themselves located near the founders' home (Carlton 1979, 16). In this situation, economic factors such as labor force considerations will be more important for the location decisions of branch plants than for single-site firms. The location of single-site firms is more a matter of chance and of personal reasons.

There is some support for this among the research discussed here, although the evidence is not overwhelming because few industrial location studies distinguish between single-site and branch plants. Most of the evidence comes from surveys, where personal reasons can be included in a list of choices, rather than statistical models which have been unable to measure "personal factors." Two surveys which investigate both single-site and branch facilities find that labor force factors were more important for branch plants. Mueller and Morgan (1962) conducted personal interviews with the managers of 230 manufacturing firms in Michigan during the early 1960s. While less than 1% of single-plant firms reported that labor force "advantages" influenced their decision to locate in Michigan, 14% of multi-plants did so (second to "personal" factors). Kieschnick (1981) surveyed companies which had made manufacturing investments over $500,000 and had considered inter-state locations. His sample was drawn from plants which had located in a state which offered an investment or employment tax credit. Even with the incentives, he finds that branch plants primarily considered the cost of skilled labor when making a state selection. Managers in single-site firms rank labor considerations behind proximity to markets, access to customers, and personal reasons.

However, the one statistical study which investigated the siting of both single-site and branch facilities found labor force factors important to both. Carlton (1979) found that the average wage rate and the unemployment rate were both significant in predicting inter-SMSA locations of new single-site firms as well as branch plants for the U.S.

Yet studies which just consider branch plant locations consistently report the importance of labor force characteristics. (No studies which only included single-site firms seem to exist. See table 2.) Fortune, Inc. (1977), Schmenner (1980), Carlton (1983), Nelson (1986), Bartik (1985), Schmenner, Huber and Cook (1987), and Johnson (1991) all investigate branch plant decisions at the state level and all report significant labor force measures. Schmenner, Bartik, and Schmenner, Huber and Cook include significant unionization and wage variables. In the Fortune, Inc. survey labor productivity ranked first; "low-cost labor" was number one for the Johnson survey. Carlton reports on the significance of wages and the unemployment rate. Nelson's back office managers discussed the importance of locating near the correct female labor force.

This leads to the fourth point. Industrial geographers have long argued that race and gender characteristics of sub-metropolitan areas play an important role in explaining industrial locations (Peck, 1989). Two surveys from this literature have looked closely at these characteristics. Nelson (1986) finds evidence that the suburbanization of clerical office work in the San Francisco SMSA is closely tied to demographic attributes of the labor force in the surrounding labor shed. Specifically, the site of back offices in the SMSA is directly related to the presence of predominantly white, native

English speaking, married with children, female labor in the area. Areas where these characteristics are more prevalent have higher numbers of back office branches. Interviews with managers of these firms supported the conclusion that they chose locations in order to be able to draw on such a labor force. Interviews done by Hanson and Pratt (1992, 381) find that businesses know, and locate to be near, inexpensive labor in the form of married female workers. About half of the interviewed firms offered flexible hours specifically to attract such women. Within the industrial location tradition Schmenner (1980) is the only study to report on the importance of gender, examining it within the context of the inter-state location decision. His surveys reveal that labor costs were of primary importance for the apparel and shoe industries, where almost all firms had located their U.S. production in low-wage areas with a ready supply of female labor. Specifically, these firms target isolated rural areas "not previously industrialized or only industrialized by industries employing overwhelmingly more men than women" (Schmenner 1980, 246). Such firms are found on the iron range in Northern Minnesota and in southern, historically textile, cities.

Kriesel and McNamara (1991) specifically model race in location decisions. They find that new plant announcements between 1986-1988 in Georgia counties was negatively related to the percent of county population that was black in 1986.

Finally, several studies look at the particular *types* of firms for which labor characteristics are most critical. Research suggests that the general availability of labor affects the location of firms across a broad range of industries, however: (1) firms locate to facilitate the hiring of appropriately-skilled labor, inasmuch as the skills they demand differ by type of industry and production process and (2) there is some evidence that larger and less capital-intensive firms are more sensitive to unionization factors than those "equipment heavy" firms that rely less on labor.

As mentioned above, Wasylenko (1980) and Erickson and Wasylenko (1980) separately model location choices for seven industrial sectors: construction; manufacturing; wholesale trade; retail trade; transportation, communications and utilities; finance, insurance and real estate; and services. An independent variable that measures current employment by place of residence for industries within commuting distance is significant for all seven sectors. Similarly, Lopez and Henderson (1989) surveyed five food processing industries regarding their choice of a site within the New England region. They report that "availability of labor" ranked in the top ten of a list of forty possible answers for four of the five: vegetable, fruit, egg, and seafood processors (it ranked 24th for poultry processors).

However, others have looked at occupational sub-classes. In Carlton (1979, 1983), where he takes a closer look at the importance of particular *kinds* of labor across three industries, he finds that the presence of engineers is relevant only for the communications equipment industry (the other two industries were fabricated plastics and electronic components). Schmenner (1980) finds that the apparel and shoe industries are in search of low-wage, lower-skilled locations, while defense contractors and communications companies go to higher skilled states such as California. Schmenner, Huber and Cook (1987) finds that the state selection for line-flow process plants (i.e., routinized production) was negatively related to the independent variable which measured the percent of the workforce having completed high school. In other words, these kinds of firms go to lower-skilled areas.

Hanson and Pratt (1991) report similar results at the municipal level in their survey of firms in three different communities in the Worchester, Massachusetts area: "Employers differed substantially from area to area in the type of labor they sought through the location decision . . " Specifically, firms employing more professionals and managers tend to locate in the higher-income Westboro area, while companies using relatively unskilled workers locate themselves in immigrant and mill-worker areas.

As expected, larger firms and labor-intensive firms are more sensitive to unionization factors. Schmenner (1980) reports that firms between the extremes of capital-intensity and labor-intensity (e.g., fabricated metals, equipment manufacturers) evidence a primary concern for labor unionization rather than wage rates. He postulates that for these types of industries, labor content is high enough to foster possible unionization, but the production process is overhauled frequently enough that union work rules would perhaps impede needed changes. Schmenner, Huber and Cook find that avoiding states with right-to-work laws varies inversely with the level of capital intensiveness (although these firms did not avoid states with high union membership). Lopez and Henderson report that while large firms ranked "labor productivity and work ethics" third in their list of location influences, small and medium firms ranked this choice 16th and 17th.

MATERIAL INPUTS

Material inputs encompass the raw and intermediate goods needed by a firm in order to produce an end product; often times these inter-firm dependencies are termed "backward linkages" (where "forward linkages" are those firms to whom one would sell). Several writers have documented the importance of such interdependence and urged local economic development practitioners to consider such linkages when targeting particular companies or industries for industrial recruitment or sectoral intervention policies. Oksanen and Williams (1984) use an input-output matrix to estimate the effects of such input and output linkages to industry location in 260 Canadian census divisions. They find that structurally dependent industries tended to cluster together by region. Anderson and Johnston (1992) discuss a method by which local development officials can use a U.S. national input-output table to analyze their local economy. They demonstrate the method by considering the linkages offered by the industrial position of large Alabama firms. Their "short list" of thirty-one possible industries to recruit included synthetic rubber, cellulosic man-made fiber, and metal barrels and drums.

Since industries vary markedly in the types of inputs needed (i.e., food processors look for animal and vegetable products, while steel manufacturers need coal and ores), it is nearly impossible for any one study of industry location to actually measure the presence of material inputs for a broad range of industries. To do so would require separate analyses by industry, so that the variable measuring input availability could vary by industry type. For most statistical models, to subset by industrial sector would leave too few "n's" to be able to estimate effects for any one industry. As a consequence, statistical models which look at a broad range of industries attempt to capture the effects of backward linkages by including a broad measure of industrial activity, such as "total employment by place of work per square mile," (which as defined includes forward linkages). The alternative is a study such as Carlton 1979 and 1983, where he focuses solely on three four-digit Standard Industrial Classification (SIC) codes (communications equipment, fabricated plastics and electronic components). As mentioned above, Erickson and Wasylenko, and Wasylenko disaggregate industries into seven one-digit SIC categories.

All but one of the statistical models in table 2 includes measures of agglomeration effects which did not distinguish between backward and

Previous Studies of Company Locations

forward linkages (Schmenner, Huber and Cook are the exceptions), and in all but Kriesel and McNamara these measures were significant. For Moses and Williamson it was "percent land in manufacturing use"; Schmenner (1978) and Charney measured it by "establishment density"; Carlton 1979 and Carlton 1983 included "production hours" for each of the three industries; Erickson and Wasylenko, and Wasylenko chose "percent of the sum of employment in the industry contained in the municipality"; Bartik looked at "production hours per square mile"; for McGuire it was "percent of the sum of workers contained in the county in which the municipality lies."

One study which considered employment growth rather than locational choice attempted a disaggregated analysis with variables measuring both input and output links. Hastings and Goode (1992) looked at the effect the availability of inputs and the market access for output had on employment trends in 20 manufacturing industries in 177 rural central places in Pennsylvania during 1965-73. The growth of fourteen of these 20 industries was positively related to the availability of inputs and the potential demand for output.

The choice between disaggregating industries or broadly defining "input supply" by measures which include "output demand" can be avoided by survey methods. Analysts may specifically ask about the importance of input availability without needing to specify the exact inputs needed. What is interesting is that, unlike the statistical models where broad measures of input availability were consistently significant, very few of the survey studies ranked the availability of inputs in a list of the top five most important concerns. Only two state-level surveys found input accessibility important: for Schmenner (1980) it ranked fourth, while for Lopez and Henderson it was second. It could be the case that other variables actually are of more concern, or perhaps the availability of inputs is so crucial to location that it is not seen as "variable." Given that other crucial factors *are* mentioned in surveys (such as access to markets and labor), it is more likely to be the case that input accessibility is less important. It is probably true that inputs remain important for the state decision, but that transportation barriers have been overcome to such an extent that inputs are considered to be available at a wide variety of sub-state locations. This is supported by the finding that none of the sub-state surveys reported a top ranking of "input availability."

ENERGY

Clearly, the availability of adequate energy availability supplies is a necessary condition at both the first- and second-level site selection stages. However, studies which report on energy considerations only exist for the state selection. Three analysts include independent variables for energy prices in econometric models (Bartik; Schmenner, Huber and Cook; and Carlton 1979 and 1983). All of these are models of the state-level location decision; this is understandable, given that energy prices are unlikely to exhibit much variation at the sub-state level. Here the evidence is inconclusive on the importance of energy prices. Neither Bartik, who measures average energy cost per BTU in manufacturing, nor Schmenner, Huber and Cook, who include average energy costs of all fuels per kilowatt hour equivalent, found the coefficients on "energy prices" significant. In fact, the signs on the coefficients for Schmenner, Huber and Cook suggest that higher-energy priced states seem to be desirable. They speculate that states with low energy costs were also perhaps too remote to be of interest (i.e., mountain or plains states with few "agglomeration economies"). Yet the studies by Carlton, where the dependent variable measures electricity prices, did conclude that energy prices were highly significant. Perhaps it is the case that the particular three industries upon which he focuses happen to be electric-dependent (fabricated plastics, communications equipment and electronic components). Or perhaps electric prices specifically are important, but including other energy inputs such as natural gas as do Bartik, and Schmenner, Huber and Cook, dilutes the influences.

Energy is rarely referred to as a location consideration in company surveys; only one survey study listed in table 2 explicitly mentions energy (Fortune 1977). Unlike the econometric studies discussed above which modeled energy *prices*, the Fortune survey asked about energy *availability*, ranking it third behind worker productivity and transportation access.

FISCAL INFLUENCES—TAXES

The current consensus in location theory is that property and income tax considerations do not influence the choice of a particular state, but do influence the intra-metropolitan decision. It is hypothesized that this difference is accounted for by the fact that at the state or regional level, any savings due to tax differentials among locations is probably overshadowed by differences in market and cost variables (Wasylenko 1981, 59). At the local level, such market and cost variables probably differ little among areas, so that tax differences have room to exert a greater impact. The studies reviewed here generally support this conclusion, although the evidence presented by statistical models is somewhat stronger than that given by surveys.

Survey evidence is mixed for both the state and local location choice. For example, in surveys considering both the state and local decision, several studies rank tax concerns in their top list of choices while others put taxes near the bottom. Taxes are ranked near the top for both decisions in the Fortune, Inc. report (where "state and local attitude toward business taxes" ranked ninth of 26), in Schmenner (1978) where taxes are listed in the top four for both stages, and in Johnson ("favorable tax climate" was classified as about sixth out of 17). Yet for Mueller and Morgan, at both levels "taxes" rank next to last; for Stafford, taxes are at the bottom of the list for all levels (including international decisions); in Schmenner (1980) taxes are listed among the bottom for the state choice and not at all for local decisions. A similar mix is found among surveys focusing on just one level of the decision. For example, Lopez and Henderson rank both income and property taxes last for state concerns, while Epping list state taxes second. The only survey to focus solely on the municipal level decision, McMillian (1965), ranks taxes third on a list of 20 factors.

However, statistical research finds fairly clear tax effects at both the state and local levels, though the effects are somewhat weaker for state decisions. For the state decision, Carlton (1979) finds that taxes exerted a significant, though small, negative impact on the location of single-site firms for the communications equipment (SIC 3662) and electronic components (3679) industries. Yet his research focusing exclusively on branches (1983), finds no significant coefficients. Bartik reports weak property tax influences (coefficients close to zero, and significant in only one of his three specifications). Schmenner, Huber and Cook likewise find inconclusive evidence for the effect of taxes (in this case, corporate tax rate, property taxes, and workmen's compensation rates) on state locations.

Much more attention has been paid to the role of taxes at the *local* level. A rich tradition in the public finance literature has explored factors influencing intraurban locations and focuses specifically on the role of municipal tax rates. Early studies in this literature find little evidence that tax rates affected industry location (Schmenner 1975, Erickson and Wasylenko 1980). However, at the suggestion of Oakland (1978), later research discovered that tax effects are masked if the sample includes places that effectively zone out industry. These places have little industry, not because of high tax rates, but because they exclude industrial land uses, and most likely among themselves have a *mix* of tax rates (thus the effect of taxes are confounded by the fact that cities with a range of tax rates have little or no industry). Studies which control for "no industry zoning" thus find significant tax effects (Wasylenko 1980, Fox 1981, McGuire 1985, McHone 1986).

SITE ATTRIBUTES

Site attributes are characteristics that are more or less "tied to the land" and are relatively immobile in the short-run. The characteristics most discussed in industrial location models are land costs and availability; infrastructure improvements; and proximity to highways and other surface transportation such as water or freight, and airports.

The evidence from both surveys and econometric models is that site attributes, as one would expect, come into play at the second decision-stage, but no one site variable consistently stands out as the most important. Site attributes are mentioned more often in local surveys than in state-level studies. For example, McMillian's municipal-level survey is the only survey in which the top four items included trucking, cost of property and land for expansion. Schmenner (1980) reports that firms put labor and market characteristics on the top of their "must have" list when selecting a state, while rail service, expressway access and utility improvements are the "must haves" at the local level. For Johnson, at both levels the top responses were labor characteristics; next in line for the state decision were state regulations, energy costs, and favorable climate--while at the local level the concerns turned to trucking connections, cost of land, and available infrastructure.

Statistical models, by design, must be more specific about attempting to gauge the effects of particular site characteristics, many of which are difficult to measure. Only one of the state-level studies reviewed here included any site attribute variables, and it was a transportation access variable. Bartik included "highway miles per square mile," which was positive and significant, which mirrors the findings for highway access variables at the metropolitan level discussed below (but the presence of highways may be as much an effect of business locations as a reason for business locations). Models of the second-stage decision contain many more site character variables.

Intrametropolitan differences in the price of land are difficult to measure, since no good source of small area land prices exists. Several authors use "distance to central city" as a proxy for prices (Moses and Williamson 1965, Schmenner 1975, Wasylenko 1980, Wasylenko 1985), where land is expected to be less expensive farther from the CBD. The results from these studies which use distance as a proxy are inconclusive and so suggest that this may not be a good proxy for land price. Moses and Williamson, and Schmenner 1975, find distance negatively (though not significantly, in the Moses and Williamson case) related to the number of new firm appearances. They speculate that the negative relationship is due to the fact that most moves are short distance moves—the farther from the CBD and from denser development, the fewer the potential movers are in proximity. That is, that most moves are short-distance moves, so the probability that any one site will be chosen is positively related to the number of potential movers nearby. Yet Erickson and Wasylenko, and Wasylenko find distance to CBD positively (though not significantly) related to the number of firms relocating from the city of Milwaukee.

Another popular approximation of land costs (and one sometimes used to proxy for labor availability, as discussed above) is some measure of land use intensity: population, employment, or housing density, where denser places are more expensive. Charney finds that population per residential acre is significant in explaining locations, particularly firms which are larger or are in the durable manufacturing sector. Erickson and Wasylenko find some evidence that "percent land in industrial use" was negatively related to firm locations, while "percent vacant land" was positively related.

Kriesel and McNamara's study was at the county level and therefore was able to avoid the "distance" proxy and instead include an estimate of "the per-acre price of the county's best industrial site." They find land price itself to be positively and significantly associated with the location of new plants. They speculate that land price represents the quality of a site (infrastructure improvements, etc.).

Together, these studies suggest that first, distance to the central business district may not a good proxy for land price because other variables of interest are related to it (e.g., distance from firm origin or site of potential movers, perhaps agglomeration economies) and thus confound the effects. Land use intensity may be better. Second, in any case land prices may not be *avoided*, as speculated, but themselves represent site quality characteristics; that is, site attributes that are *sought.*

Transportation access variables are somewhat easier to measure and have more consistent results. Moses and Williamson, and Erickson and Wasylenko include a 0,1 dummy "access to interstate highway" which is positive and significant; the same is true for Kriesel and McNamara's "# of highway miles" and Charney's "distance to highway." Railroad access seems not to matter for those studies which considered it: neither Schmenner (1975) nor Charney find "railroad" effects. However, there is some evidence that the importance of highway access to business locations has waned in recent years (Forkenbrock and Foster 1996).

Finally to be discussed are infrastructure improvements. Kriesel and McNamara, as discussed, speculate that higher land prices were associated with site improvements and did find a significant coefficient for this variable. Erickson and Wasylenko found no association between "per capita expenditures on sanitation services" and firm location. Charney, who included "sewer acres/land" did find such an association. She speculates that her variable was a more accurate measure of availability than that used by Erickson and Wasylenko, because costs of providing services can vary among areas.

MARKET FACTORS

Location theory holds that market factors (proximity to customers) are more important to the choice of a particular region or state (that is, influence the first-stage decision) than to the choice of a particular municipality. Firms tend to choose a region that meets their market needs, and then choose a "best" low-cost site within that region (Greenhut 1956, Schmenner 1982). Several of the survey studies under review here support this conclusion. For example, in Stafford's ranking of state and local decisions, market accessibility is listed third for the state decision and thirteenth (next-to-last) for the local decision. In Schmenner's 1980 study, firms rank proximity to markets second on a list of state-level influences, and not at all for site choices. Market proximity is fourth on Lopez and Henderson's list of 26 factors.

Markets are also more important to single-site firms than to branch operations. Kieschnick, who studied branches and single-site companies, finds that markets ranked first for one-site firms and thirteenth for branches. Branch operations in Johnson's study ranked markets near the middle of a 25 point ranking for both state and local decisions. The reason for this difference seems clear. Branch operations "feed into" the parent company, are not usually the primary point of sales, and often ship their output to other branches of the same firm rather than to customers.

However, the market area for products and services (customers) will be different for firms in different industries. Business services are less export-oriented than markets for intermediate and final goods; therefore one would expect business service firms to position themselves closer to potential customers than firms in other industries.

The evidence given by statistical studies on the importance of market factors can not be as clear, because "market access" is not easily quantified for firms in a range of industrial sectors. Industry-specific characteristics such as proximity to customers may be directly inquired about in a survey, without needing to specify the exact nature of customers, while statistical models must somehow approximate these characteristics with quantifiable variables. The most common proxy for market access are measures of existing industrial activity (usually employment or establishment densities). Yet these are also the measures used to approximate "input availability" (see section above), so that the relative importance of these two factors cannot be disentangled. Measures of existing industrial activity were significant in all but one of the statistical studies in which it was included.

PERSONAL FACTORS

Personal factors refer to *chance* factors such as proximity to owner's home, knowledge of area through personal contacts, etc.; and to *quality of life* factors such as climate, good housing, schools, cultural activities, low crime etc. Early industrial location literature focused essentially on cost and market factors, but the importance of personal factors has been increasingly investigated since the early 1970s (Isard 1975). As with some of the other characteristics reviewed above, surveys are a better instrument by which to investigate the importance of personal factors than are statistical models. To include data in a model on chance factors such as proximity to owner's home, availability of personal contacts, etc., would most likely require performing a survey anyway, and answers may not be all that amenable to quantification. Therefore the most information we have about chance factors come from survey studies.

Chance factors especially seem to play a larger role in the location of firms than previously thought. For example, in Stafford's survey, "personal contacts" tops the list for both the regional and local decision. Often firm managers will cite rational factors upon which they think a location decision ought to be made, but when asked about an actual location choice they themselves had made in the past, historical accident and personal contacts are cited more frequently.

The type of firm most influenced by chance factors are smaller, and tend to be new companies or single-site firms. Blair and Premus (1987, 73) note in their review essay that "new businesses are less sensitive to the profit-maximizing aspects of locational choice than branch plants." Mueller and Morgan (1962, 207) report that ". . . personal considerations and historical accident play a much greater role in the location of factories of smaller firms than in the location of factories which are part of larger multiplant firms."

The information we have about quality of life characteristics is also primarily from surveys. Even though quantifiable proxies for "quality of life" status are available, such as school expenditures, income levels, etc., few models have included variables which attempt to capture quality of life considerations. A few exceptions are noted below.

What the evidence reveals is that a set of "quality of life factors" come into play during the state decision, while others are more important for the intra-metropolitan site choice. For example, the role of amenities such as climate, outdoor recreational opportunities and a lack of urban congestion are seen as increasingly important to high technology industries wishing to attract high-skilled labor (Gottlieb 1995). Schmenner, Huber and Cook found that "mean January temperature" was associated with location choice (probably not a proxy for "southern states without labor unionism," since they controlled for state right-to-work status). On the whole, though, we may expect that local amenities influence the local decision rather more so than state choices. Firms most likely choose a state for market and other more broad-based factors, then let local quality of life characteristics affect their choice of a particular site. Stafford finds, for example, that local amenities climbed the list of important factors as the region under consideration narrowed. For the local choice, amenities were 3rd on a list of 15. One attempt to model amenities at the intra-metropolitan level here is Charney, who included "high-income households" as an independent variable. In her case, the coefficient was negative, either because high-income communities zone out or let housing outbid industrial sites; or because firms need lower-wage labor than that available in these types of communities. Other variables may be better approximations for quality of life considerations.

SUMMARY

The preceding discussion indicates that evidence for the importance of labor force factors to the industrial location decision has been given by a wealth of previous research. The evidence seems to suggest that labor force factors come into play for companies when they are choosing the broad region or state in which to locate ("first stage decisions") and when they choose the particular city and site ("second stage decisions"). At the first stage, businesses compare wage rates and unionization factors, while at the second stage they consider the availability of the particular kind of labor force they need. For some businesses, the gender of the labor force is an important attribute, for example for companies looking for stable clerical workers. This suggests that if the gender of a labor force affects the siting of economic activity, it will play a role in second-stage, local, decisions. Second-stage decisions are also characterized by an interest in other site factors such as proximity to transportation and tax rates. We should see evidence for the importance of these factors in this study here of company site decisions among suburban municipalities within Chicago.

The research reviewed here also indicated that economic factors, which include worker characteristics, are more important for the location decisions of branch plants than for single-site firms. The siting of single-site firms is said to be more a matter of chance and personal reasons. New firms tend to be formed as the opportunity arises, perhaps near the founders' home. In this case, there may be no relation between typical location factors and the siting of the firm, because the firm was located fortuitously and not with any specific location considerations as a priority. This suggests that if female workers is important to the location decision of a firm, that firm is more likely to be a branch firm, the focus of the study here, than a single-site company.

But *how* important are women workers to the siting of businesses in the suburbs? More important than transportation accessibility, or land costs, etc.? This review of previous research suggests that workers are one of many factors reviewed by firms when choosing locations. The studies which have concentrated on exploring labor force considerations have usually not paid as close attention to other factors, partly because they were written by industrial geographers trying to fill a gap in previous research as was discussed in chapter 1. The focus of these studies is an effort to understand the labor process rather than an attempt to examine the relative importance of workers as a factor in company location (e.g., Hanson and Pratt 1995). Yet these studies remain the primary source of information on the importance of labor to industrial location.

It is possible to combine the emphasis on workers with other studies of business site choices that highlight traditional factors such as business costs and market accessibility. In the first place, research on traditional factors does not altogether ignore labor factors, although it does tend to stress labor costs and general accessibility rather than give rich evidence on the types of labor for which firms are looking--evidence afforded by labor geographers. Secondly, by using both a survey and a statistical model, this book may offer the econometric rigor employed most often by traditional location theorists, but adding some of the detail appreciated by industrial geographers.

Given this overview of research, we can expect that women workers play a significant role in branch plant location decisions when these plants are choosing among cities. Most likely, the survey will reveal that labor force factors in general will rank among the top four reasons given by firms, along

Previous Studies of Company Locations

with proximity to markets, transportation access, and land cost and availability.

The statistical model will include significant labor force factors, even when including measures of city size and agglomeration factors in order to parcel out the independent effect of labor availability. Are the firms attracted to levels of population and industrial activity, or is it specifically labor? For industrial activity, because the survey can ask firm- and industry-specific information, it can report on the relevance of input-output linkages (which varies by firm, so is not amenable to statistical models). The statistical model includes measures of general urbanization and industrial activity.

Tax rates should also be significant. But, as Oakland's (1978) suggests, some cities will zone out industrial development and thus should be controlled for. The statistical model presented later thus presents likely variables associated with cities which would be prone to zone out development, such as industrial equalized assessed value, housing density, and income levels. Finally, a set of other site attributes which the literature suggests are second-stage factors are also included: transportation access, land cost and availability, access to markets, and quality of life considerations. Measures of each are included in the model, and are inquired about in the survey. Quality of life considerations are difficult to measure, however, and the primary source of information regarding the relative importance of this factor will be the survey.

The following chapter describes the methods by which data were gathered. Described are both the survey of businesses, variables gathered as proxies for location factors. The chapter also specifies the model equations used.

III
Data and Method

To explore the importance of labor force characteristics and other location factors to the company location decision, two general approaches were used: a statistical model, using variables from a *municipal database*, and a survey of firms. This chapter discusses how the database and survey were designed and how the data were collected, with reference to how these methods were used by other studies. As was reported in the previous chapter, this study is one of the first of its kind to look into the firm location decision by both surveying firms and by also using a statistical model.

WHY BOTH A SURVEY AND A MODEL?

By employing both a survey and a model, this study uses the advantages of each method to overcome the disadvantages of using only one or the other method. Surveys, for example, offer advantages in several respects. First, they can describe the importance of the role of factors which influence location decisions but are difficult or impossible to quantify. Such "difficult to quantify" variables can include personal reasons such as "we wanted to locate near the owner's home," and factors whose specific characteristic will vary for firms in diverse industries, such as "availability of inputs" where the particular inputs needed will vary for different companies. In addition, surveys offer the researcher the opportunity to ask open-ended questions and thus perhaps identify factors not thought of in advance.

However, the validity of survey response answers has often been called into question. Answers to survey questions may be influenced by a firm's desire to sway development policy in their favor. For example, firms may report that a city subsidy or tax rates biased their decision to choose one municipality over another, in the hopes of affecting the availability of subsidies or the future level of taxes. For location decisions made far in the past, the memory of what affected location choices has faded, and responses are guesses based on what is perceived to be important to the firm's current operation. Another likely shortcoming is that often it is difficult to identify or find the person(s) responsible for making the decision. This person may have left the firm, or perhaps more than one person was responsible for making the location choice. The latter situation would require that more than one person be identified and participate in filling out the survey, a more costly and time consuming task.

In addition, mail surveys suffer in that likely responses must be identified ahead of time so that they can appear as alternatives from which to choose. Although open-ended questions can be included as well, respondents are unlikely to write in answers (Dillman 1978, 58). Answers to open-ended questions may be biased in that those who do respond are likely to feel especially strongly about the question, while those for whom the same open-ended answer applies, but do not feel strongly, are not counted. Some of this problem may be overcome with pre-testing to help assure that as many relevant choices as possible are identified ahead of time.

Statistical models, on the other hand, offer the advantage of being able to specify the size and direction of relationships among factors and particular dependent variables which would be difficult to inquire about in a survey—population density, for an example. W may want to know whether population density drives out development, but a survey question worded "did you avoid cities with high population densities?" would be awkward. Yet models can be disadvantageous in that all perceived factors (independent variables) must be quantifiable. Analysts find themselves in the unenviable position of finding existing data that might measure subjective factors such as "quality of life," or of approximating somewhat quantifiable variables by the best available measure (e.g., "employment density" is used in many models as a proxy for "the availability of companies which may supply inputs"). One is not always sure whether the measure really captures the essence of the variable it is meant to estimate.

Since surveys and statistical models each have shortcomings, both methods are used here to study the location decisions of businesses. What the survey does is allow a more finely-tuned exploration of the kinds of firms for which differing factors matter, while the model affords the ability to

Data and Method   41

explore overall relationships. In addition, each methodology can be used to flesh out questions raised by the other. For example, the survey answers can be used to explore inconclusive estimates from the statistical model, while the municipal database and statistical model affords the opportunity to explore the meaning behind survey responses.

SUBURBAN CITIES AND FIRMS

The Cities

This study included all municipalities over 2500 population in 1990 located in the six-county Chicago metropolitan area (Cook, DuPage, Lake, McHenry, Kane, and Will counties), outside the city of Chicago.[1] Of the 203 cities so identified, 149 were later found to be home to one or more branches (the identification of branch locations is discussed in the next section). Thus, this study is a study of businesses who chose suburban locations, and why they chose those locations. It does not include companies in the city, and so cannot directly answer the question of why some businesses might chose city sites. It instead can better address the question of what is particularly attractive about suburban locations.

The Firms

The universe of 1302 firms was identified by using Dun and Bradstreet's *Dun's Market Indicators* (DMI) data for 1992. The Dun and Bradstreet company collects information on businesses as part of its role as a credit rating agency but became more aggressive in seeking out firms in the mid-1980s. The new strategy was part of an attempt to create a comprehensive list of businesses, including firms not necessarily seeking a credit rating. DMI listings have been used by state and local business development organizations as well as economic researchers to identify individual firms or track local economic activity (Birch 1987, Aldrich et al. 1989). The list, although more comprehensive than other available listings, suffers in that it is somewhat less accurate (Carlson 1995).[2]

   The list from Dun and Bradstreet contained a list of 5833 companies. These 5833 firms were branch establishments, in any kind of industry, located in the six county Chicago metropolitan area outside the city of

Chicago itself. No restriction was placed on the location of the headquarters. Through several steps these 5833 records became a "working universe" of 1302 firms (table 3). The universe of 1302 firms was obtained by deleting duplicate listings, omitting companies that were in cities that were not included in the study, and eliminating "consumer-oriented" and "resource-oriented" firms. Consumer-oriented operations such as transportation and public utilities, retail, wholesale, personal services, banking, education, and government were excluded because the location of these industrial sectors is dictated almost entirely by the demand for their services by people, rather than by traditional "economic development" factors such as labor accessibility, taxes, etc. Also excluded were industries that are entirely dependent on inputs and so are not free to move around based on the attractiveness of other location factors (agriculture and mining), and the construction industry, where production is at many sites.

Other cleaning procedures were also performed. Using street maps (American Map Corporation 1993), a geocoding process was performed to make sure that the address given on the Dun and Bradstreet file was actually physically situated in the city given by the postal code (173 firms were re-assigned municipalities). In addition, duplicate listings were eliminated after the geocoding process.

About 66% of the final list of branches and employment is concentrated in manufacturing industries with the remainder in business services (table 3). The average size of a manufacturing establishment is only slightly larger than that of a business service firm (160 vs.156 employees). Experience suggests that manufacturing firms should be much bigger than business service companies, but several large firms in SIC Code 873 (research and testing services, where the average firm size is 584 employees) contribute to a high overall average employment for services.

These 1302 firms are found in 149 of the 203 possible suburban cities (appendix 1 lists cities, branch firms and employment, and population). These 149 cities are clustered near the central city and in several outlying older industrial centers such as Aurora-Joliet and Elgin (figures 1 and 2 depict the spatial distribution of branches and branch employment). The areas of largest concentration of branch activity are clustered along the interstate highway system, forming the "backward C" shape of economic activity.

Table 3
Branch Firms By Standard Industrial Classification Code

SIC Code	Industry Name	# Firms	Employment
20	Food and kindred products	62	12,946
21	Tobacco products	1	333
22	Textile mill products	4	160
23	Apparel and other textile products	5	705
24	Lumber and wood products	5	168
25	Furniture and fixtures	18	1,805
26	Paper and allied products	50	5,726
27	Printing and publishing	81	7,978
28	Chemicals and allied products	102	11,186
29	Petroleum and coal products	10	1,585
30	Rubber and misc. plastics products	68	7,065
32	Stone, clay and glass products	45	4,987
33	Primary metal industries	43	5,521
34	Fabricated metal products	86	12,441
35	Industrial machinery and equipment	104	25,637
36	Electronic & electrical equipment	87	27,836
37	Transportation equipment	12	3,298
38	Instruments and related products	45	5,007
39	Miscellaneous manufacturing indust.	23	2,505
	Manufacturing total	851	136,889
731	Advertising	7	314
732	Credit reporting and collection	12	908
733	Mailing, reproduction, stenographic	15	995
734	Services to buildings	12	634
735	Misc. equipment rental and leasing	26	1,333
736	Personnel supply services	11	1,410
737	Computer and data processing	76	6,823
738	Miscellaneous business services	89	12,361
871	Engineering & architectural services	41	6,109
872	Accounting, auditing, bookkeeping	26	2,095
873	Research and testing services	44	25,716
874	Management and public relations	92	11,664
	Services total	451	70,362

FIGURE 1
NUMBER OF FIRMS BY MUNICIPALITY

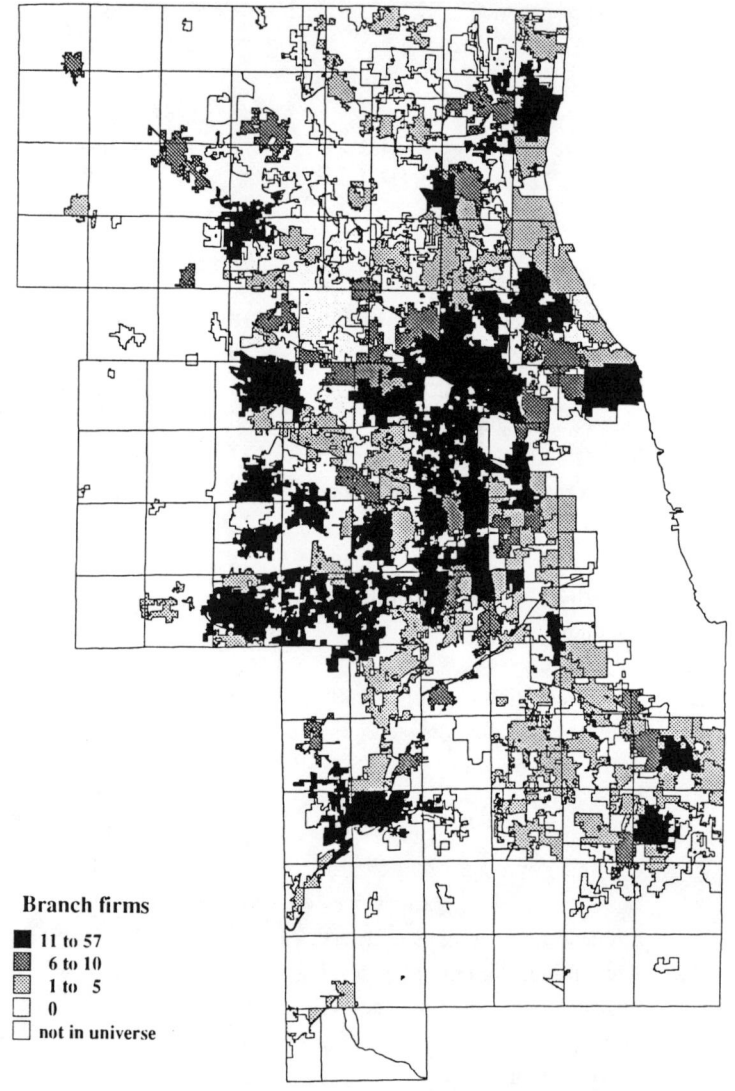

FIGURE 2
BRANCH EMPLOYMENT BY MUNICIPALITY

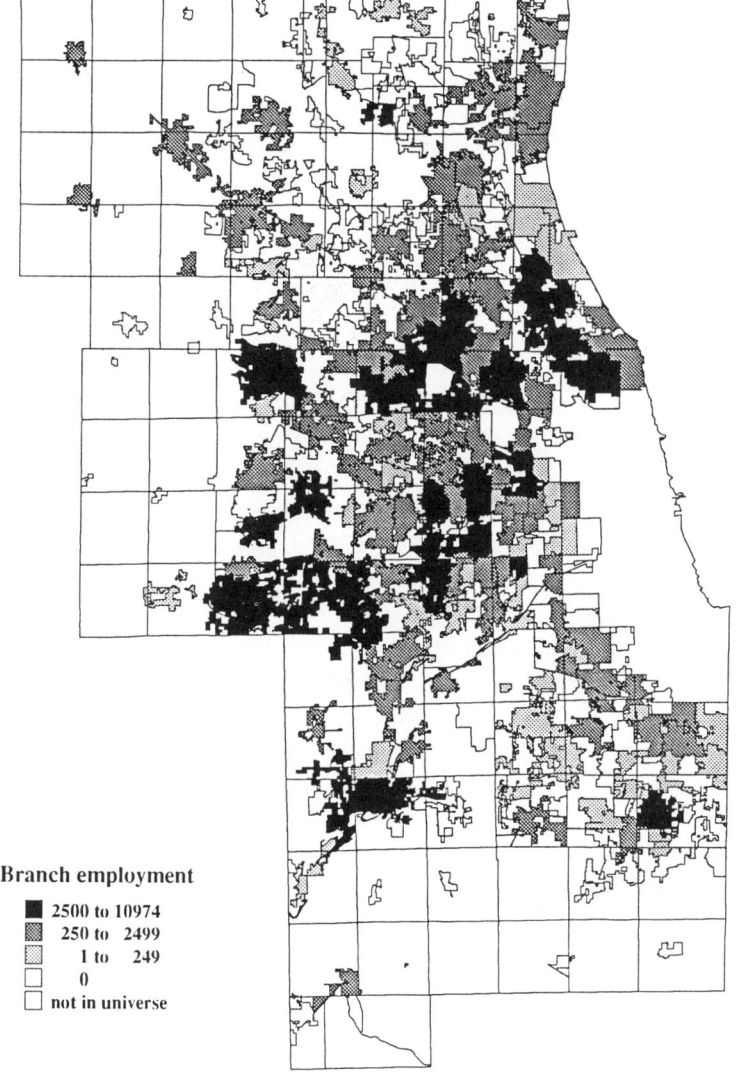

As would be expected, cities with many firms are also cities with large employment levels. The exceptions seem to occur among cities along the North Shore (such as Evanston) which have many firms but less employment (so, smaller firms on average), while suburbs to the west have few firms but much employment. There are also a few far north and northwest suburbs which have smaller-than-average firms (from right to left): Waukegan, Mundelein, and Crystal Lake. The south suburbs are noteworthy in the general lack of activity when compared to the rest of the metropolitan area.

Several inner-ring northwest suburbs top the list in terms of branch locations: Elk Grove Village, Schaumburg, and Des Plaines. But the larger employment centers tend to be cities farther from Chicago's central business district (CBD) with historically more room for expansion: Naperville, Rolling Meadows, and Aurora.

THE STATISTICAL MODEL AND MUNICIPAL DATABASE

As mentioned previously, this study used both a statistical model and a survey to explore the reasons for businesses choosing particular sites. Let us first turn our attention to the nature of the statistical model, including the rationale for choosing particular variables and the nature of the actual data collected.

The branch activity located in a city, we may speculate, is the outcome of the quantity and quality of the sites available, and other business amenities attached to the city and site as discussed in the previous chapter. Therefore, from the review in the previous chapter, a complete statistical model which would accurately predict the quantity of branch activity in any one city would need to account for such variables as the size of the city, the availability and quality of land, infrastructure, labor, and other inputs; the costs of doing business such as tax rates; amenities and quality of life characteristics; and the city's receptiveness to commercial and industrial development. In general, the model can be symbolized as follows:

Data and Method

Q_m = f(city size and site availability, city location and access, city characteristics, proximity to other businesses, tax rates, site quality, labor force characteristics)

However, the quantity of branch activity located in different cities can be measured in different ways. Do we mean total employment, or total firms? Or, just business services? Or, manufacturing? Therefore, six different measures of activity (our *dependent* variables) will be used:

Q_m = the quantity of branch activity in municipality *m*
NUM (Number of branch firms)
EMP (Employment)
BSRVNUM (Number of business service firms)
BSRVEMP (Business service employment)
MFGNUM (Number of manufacturing firms)
MFGEMP (Manufacturing employment)

The *independent* variables, or factors that we expect will predict the level of branch activity in suburbs, are measured using the following variables:

city size and site availability =
SQKILM (Land area in kilometers miles in 1980)
CPOP1000 (City population 1980 in 1,000)
POP_DEN (City population density)
city location and access =
HGHWAY1 (Highway accessible from ramp)
HGHWAY2 (Highway accessible within 2 miles)
HGHWAY3 (Highway accessible 2-5 miles)
OHARE1 (City 2-5 miles from airport)
OHARE2 (City >2 to 10 miles from airport)
OHARE3 (City >10 miles from airport)
TOLOOP (Distance to Chicago's CBD, called "The Loop")
city characteristics =
CITYAGE (Age of city in years)
CPBLACK (Percent Black population 1980)
MHSINC (Median household income)

tax rates =
  MUNI81 (Municipal tax rate)
  EFRATE81 (Effective tax rate)
    available for a subset of 108 cities
site quality =
  CAPOUT82 (Municipal capital expenditures/land area)
    available for a subset of 103 cities
labor force =
  FEM_DEN (Density of surrounding women with kids)
  ELEM_DEN (Density of surrounding elementary grads)
  COL_DEN (Density of surrounding college grads)
  MEN_DEN (Density of surrounding men 18-44)
proximity to other businesses =
  STOTDEN8 (Density of surrounding employment 1981)
  SMFGDEN8 (Density of surrounding mfg. emp. 1981)

The Dependent Variables

The six dependent variables are used in the statistical equations presented in the next chapter: (1) total firms, (2) total employment, (3) manufacturing firms, (4) manufacturing employment, (5) business service firms, and (6) business service employment (a description of these and the independent variables are presented in table 4 below). However, as mentioned above, only 149 of the 203 cities were home to branch firms. This means that a large portion (about 27%) of the cities have *no* branches located in their borders. Since statistical models have difficulty dealing with data that is "bottom heavy" (lots of values at the low end of the scale, or *positively skewed* in statistical terms) as are these data, we must transform the data so that all values cluster closer to the bottom, where the value for so many cities fall. To do this, we can instead use the log of the values in each of these variables, rather than the real value. The interpretation of the output from this model is then a little different, as will be explained later.

The Independent Variables

The second set of variables, the independent variables, includes all those factors that we suspect are associated with varying amounts of firm locations in cities and are explained in detail below. These independent variables,

Data and Method

representing expected influences on branch activity, were measured in 1980 or as close to 1980 as possible. The count of branch firms and employment (the dependent variables) are from 1992, so that the independent variables are conceived as factors affecting firm decisions to locate or remain in the city during the 1980s. The "short form" of the variable name is given in parentheses immediately following the title; for reference, all means and standard deviations are given in table 4 below.

A Note on Surrounding Cities

Some economic factors which influence where a firm may elect to locate really are attributes of a larger area surrounding the municipality as well as the municipality itself. For example, the labor available to a firm in any city is not just the labor force located in that city. Rather, labor comes from the city itself as well as the surrounding area. The same may be said of variables which attempt to capture agglomeration economies, land density, etc.

Therefore, some variables are measured not just for the "home" city, but for that city and all surrounding cities (out to a five mile radius). A city was considered to be a "surrounding city" if any portion of that city was within 5 miles of the home city. The five-mile criterion was chosen to reflect the median commute time and distance for workers in the Chicago suburbs in 1990, since the majority of these "surrounding" variables consist of worker characteristics.[3]

Yet to do so for each of our 203 cities would have been impossible. Using cities as the basis for defining surrounding areas, rather than smaller areas such as census tracts (which would have been impossible) has implications for the construction of variables based on the definition of surrounding areas. First, because by definition unincorporated areas are not within municipal boundaries, activity in unincorporated areas is not included in any variables based on "city plus surrounding area." Second, the areas coded as "surrounding" differed because we designated a city as "surrounding" if *any* portion was within the circumference of the 5-mile circle. Therefore the total *area* coded as "surrounding" differs by city, depending on the size of surrounding cities and the presence of unincorporated areas. To correct for this, variables using surrounding areas are standardized by land area. This is explained in more detail in the "labor force" section below. Using density to standardize labor force variables was also used by Wasylenko (1980) and Erickson and Wasylenko (1980).

City Size and Site Availability

Land Area 1980 (*SQKILM*)
This is defined as land area, in square kilometers, within the municipal boundaries in 1980. It is included in the model in order to control for the sheer size of a city. Cities with more land area, all else equal, will have more branch firms and employment. This variable was taken from the 1980 Census of Population and Housing (Census of Population and Housing 1980).

Population 1980 (*CPOP1000*)
Population is measured as the population of the municipality (in 1000s) as reported in the 1980 Census (Census of Population and Housing 1980). As with land area, population is included in the model as a measure of city size. Some studies which include industries that sell to local consumer markets (i.e., retail and wholesale firms) in their analyses have used "population" as an indicator of potential consumer demand (Wasylenko 1980, McGuire 1985). However, for the manufacturing and business service firms examined in this study, population serves as a measure of general municipal activity that would foster firm locations. For example, places with larger populations for a given land area are more likely to have needed infrastructure improvements; established public safety organizations; development departments located in city government; residential amenities such as public libraries, shopping and theaters; and etc.

Population Density of City 1980 (*POP_DEN*)
Investigation of a graph of the relationship between population and branch activity suggests that branch activity declines as population grows. That is, the graphs suggest that a certain level of population is desired but that higher densities drive out development. The model thus includes both city population and population density of the city and surrounding area. Population density of the city and surrounding area is expected to put pressure on the price and availability of land for industrial development within a city, and so be negatively correlated with branch locations. It is likely that at lower population levels the presence of people suggests an attractive amount of municipal development, while higher population densities indicate potential problems such as competition between industrial and residential land uses, higher levels of congestion, etc.

Table 4
Descriptive Statistics for Variables

Variable		Mean	Standard Deviation	N
NUM	# firms (log=LNUM)	6.44	9.98	203
EMP	Employment (log=LEMP)	1020.97	1850.05	203
BSRVNUM	# business service firms (log=LBSRVNUM)	2.27	4.91	203
BSRVEMP	Business service emp. (log=LBSRVEMP)	346.66	1123.65	203
MFGNUM	# manufacturing firms (log=LMFGNUM)	4.23	6.52	203
MFGEMP	Manufacturing employment (log=LMFGEMP)	674.36	1331.73	203
SQKILM	Land area in square kilometers	5.26	4.55	203
CPOP1000	City population in 1,000	16.24	15.98	203
POP_DEN	Surrounding population density	3.34	1.40	203
HGHWAY1	Highway accessible from ramp	.34	.47	203
HGHWAY2	Highway accessible within 2 miles	.13	.34	203
HGHWAY3	Highway accessible 2-5 miles	.18	.38	203
OHARE1	City 2-5 miles from airport	.03	.17	203
OHARE2	City >2 to 10 miles from airport	.20	.40	203
TOLOOP	Distance to Chicago's CBD	28.24	12.16	203
CITYAGE	Age of city in years	76.37	30.85	203
CPBLACK	Percent city Black population	4.58	16.39	203
STOTDEN8	5-mile total emp./land area	1254.40	800.47	203
SMFGDEN	5-mile mfg employment/land	406.72	331.65	203
MHSINC	Median household income	26.90	8.67	203
MUNI81	Tax rate levied by municipality	1.11	.67	203
EFRATE81	Effective tax rate 1981	3.87	1.66	108
CAPOUT82	City capital outlays/land area	156.20	213.13	103
FEM_DEN	5-mile density women w/kids	697.51	274.99	203
MEN_DEN	5-mile density men 18-44	517.17	189.45	203
COL_DEN	5-mile density college grads	270.96	146.51	203
ELEM_DEN	5-mile density elementary grads	572.49	346.55	203

City Location and Access

Highway Access (*HIGHWAYx*)

Highway access was measured as a series of 0,1 (no, yes) "dummy" variables which measured the distance to the nearest highway entrance ramp using a major feeder street: HGHWAY1 (an entrance ramp is located within the municipal boundaries); HGHWAY2 (driving on a major feeder gives access to an entrance ramp in less than 2 miles); HGHWAY3 (driving on a major feeder gives access to an entrance ramp within 2 to 5 miles); and, HGHWAY4 (access is over 5 miles away). The means in table 4 indicate that 34% of the 1302 companies are located in cities with a highway entrance ramp; 13% are in cities where an entrance ramp is located less than 2 miles away.

To give some room for variation in the estimation (i.e., to allow the underlying simultaneous equations in the regression to be uniquely soluble), only HGHWAY1, HGHWAY2 and HGHWAY3 are included in the model. It is expected that cities with better access to highways will attract more development. This variable was coded by hand with reference to six-county road maps (Chicago Tribune-Rand McNally 1992). The question is, perhaps, how close firms like to be.

Proximity to O'Hare Airport (*OHAREx*)

Proximity to O'Hare Airport was also measured as a series of 0,1 dummy variables measured in concentric rings (that is, "as the crow flies," not road miles) whose center is the airport itself: OHARE1 (city was 0-2 miles from the airport); OHARE2 (city was greater than 2 to 10 miles); and OHARE3 (city is greater than 10 miles from the airport). Again, to allow mathematical estimation, only OHARE1 and OHARE2 are entered in the model. This variable was coded by hand using a six-county area map (Chicago Tribune-Rand McNally 1992) and compass.

Proximity to the airport will most likely be associated with more branch locations, but perhaps not because companies are looking for access to air transportation. Although some firms may use the airport facilities (for example, business service firms may want passenger travel, while some industrial firms may need freight service), some research suggests that land near airports is undesirable for residential use and thus priced or zoned for business development. Thus it may not be airport access per se, but instead the effect the airport has on surrounding land uses that spurs nearby

Data and Method

industrial and commercial development. Indeed, since the variable measures distance not with respect to road access but purely in terms of proximity to the airport, this variable is a better measure of the effect of the airport land use on surrounding land uses and prices than of the effect of airport accessibility.

Distance to Chicago's Central Business District (*TOLOOP*)

The distance to Chicago's central business district ("the Loop") was taken from values given on the Chicago Tribune-Rand McNally Chicagoland map (Chicago Tribune-Rand McNally 1992). Again, these are values independent of roadways (i.e., "as the crow flies"). Distance to the Loop is used here as a proxy for several concepts. First, previous research suggests that wages and land prices decline with distance to the central business district (Muth 1969, Mills 1972). Second, more businesses have historically been situated nearer the central city, and thus cities closer to Chicago will have more to offer in the way of agglomeration economies (suppliers and buyers). Finally, research by Moses and Williamson (1967) and by Schmenner (1978) suggests that when businesses relocate, most moves are short-distance moves (less than 6 miles). Due to day-to-day casual contacts, companies are better informed and feel more comfortable about cities and sites near their present location than about possible locations further away. They will thus tend to choose from a nearby set of sites, which are known, and are less apt to seek out the unfamiliar. Given that at any one time more businesses are near the central business district, it follows that most moves will be to other cities near the central business district (although perhaps a few miles further away).

City Characteristics
Race (*CPBLACK*)
This is measured as those persons reporting themselves as "Black" on the 1980 Census (Census table 12), less persons of Hispanic origin reporting themselves as "Black" (Census table 14) as a percent of total city population. We might expect that firms will tend to avoid cities with high minority populations because of discrimination and the historical effects of discrimination (crime, disinvestment in infrastructure, etc.).

Median Household Income 1980 (*MHSINC*)
There are two reasons for expecting the relation between higher median household income and branch locations to be negative. First, labor is more expensive, either because local labor costs more or firms have to pay a premium to workers who must commute from farther. Second, higher income communities are more likely to zone out development. Yet the relation may be positive for those firms which desire the local amenities afforded by communities with higher incomes. Probably industrial firms will display the negative and commercial firms will exhibit a positive relationship. The next chapter, which presents findings for the entire set of branch firms and for the industrial and commercial firms separately, will flesh this out. This variable was taken from the 1980 Census of Population and Housing.

Age of City (*CITYAGE*)
"Age of city" is a proxy for city type. City age is one way to distinguish between newer suburbs and older industrial towns. Such older towns, especially in the Chicago area, are more likely to be those with an historically independent industrial economic base, while newer towns may be more likely to be residential suburbs or have sprung from office development. In this case, older towns are more likely to have been hospitable to manufacturing development. This variable captures a crucial part of the relationship between municipal factors and location decisions and this study is the first to include such a measure. The value of this variable is the number of years since the certificate of incorporation was issued by the Secretary of State (Illinois, Secretary of State, 1991).

Proximity to Other Businesses
Employment Density (*STOTDEN8* and *SMFGDEN8*)
This variable takes the form:

total employment in 5-mile cities / total land area in 5-mile cities

where total employment is place-of-work payroll employment taken from *Where Workers Work* (Illinois Department of Employment Security 1981).[4] Land area is used to standardize total employment for the reasons outlined in the "Labor Force" section above: due to the inexactness of coding

Data and Method 55

"surrounding areas," not all surrounding areas are in fact the same land area. This measure is included along with population density in order to avoid the problem encountered by McGuire (1985), whereby she could not ultimately distinguish between the effects of labor force factors and agglomeration economies.

Cities with more dense development may be cities which are generally favorable to development. In addition, more dense development is an indication of several of the same economic variables as is distance to central business district (discussed above) but some of these variables may have a "push-pull" influence on firm location. For example, the more dense is overall employment, the more proximate will be other businesses. The presence of such agglomeration economies should exert a positive influence on branch locations. However, more densely developed municipalities will exhibit more competition for, and thus affect the availability and price of, land and labor. This, then, will exert a negative influence on branch locations.

Tax Rates (*MUNI81* and *EFRATE81*)

Property tax rates differ for parcels within cities depending on the rates for various special districts which overlap municipal boundaries—i.e., the school districts, townships, and sometimes county in which the parcel lies. For example, a single city may lie within two or three different high school districts, each of which levies a different rate. Furthermore, the ratio of assessed value to market value (the assessment/sales price ratio, or ASSP ratio) differs among counties; a property worth $100,000 may be assessed at $33,000 in one county and $24,000 in another.

Equalization factors also play a role in causing tax rates to differ among municipal properties. Properties of different types is assessed at different rates within any one county. For example, in Cook county, the central county of the Chicago metropolitan area, residential property of 6 units or less is assessed at 16% of market value while industrial and commercial property is assessed at 40%. State statute mandates that the assessment/sales price ratio for a county as a whole must be 33%. To adjust for differences in ASSP ratios by property type, the Illinois Department of Revenue imposes what is known as an "equalization factor" to assessed values. This factor differs by property type. The equalization factor brings the assessment ratio for all properties in the county to 33%. In the collar counties, ASSP ratios do not differ so much by property type, and equalization factors are close to 1.0.

Statutory tax rates thus do not reflect the real differences in property taxes paid by the owners of property of equal value among municipalities. To construct an accurate municipal-level property tax rate one would need to take a weighted average of tax rates in overlapping districts, multiply the resulting rate by the county assessment/sales price ratio (calculated separately for cities which cross county boundaries), and finally multiply by the equalization factor. An appropriate weighting variable would be some measure of municipal property located in the district—equalized assessed value, perhaps, or land area if EAV by district is not available. Such a rate is called an *effective tax rate*.

Unfortunately for the project discussed here, such information on overlapping districts is only available in Illinois for cities over 10,000 population. Since this project included cities over 2,500 people, effective tax rates could not be calculated for the entire set of cities. Another measure, the municipal tax rate (MUNI81) was used. A second analysis just of cities over 10,000, which uses the effective tax rate (EFRATE81) is also presented. The results differ somewhat, given that the municipal tax rate and the effective tax rate is only slightly related (the Pearson's R^2 between municipal tax rate and effective tax rate for the cities here is .25). EFRATE81 was available for a subset of 108 cities.

Effective tax rates were estimated using five major overlapping districts for each municipality—county, township, municipality, elementary school district, and high school district. These rates were weighted by land area (the percent of municipal land area contained in the district). The sum of these weights for each type of district was 100%. Land area was approximated by visually referencing municipal maps available from the Illinois State Library.[5] Each rate was then multiplied by its "land percent" and summed by type. The sum of types is the aggregate rate. The aggregate rate was then multiplied by the appropriate industrial (not residential) assessment/sales price ratio and equalization factor (Illinois Department of Revenue 1981). For example, 60% of Elmhurst city in 1981 was located in Addison township (tax rate = 0.153) and 40% in York township (tax rate = 0.195). However, the entire city was located in unit school district 205 (tax rate 4.117). Its weighted township tax rate for 1981 is thus 0.1698 ([.6 x 0.153] + [.4 x 0.195]), while its high school rate is 4.117. Other district rates were

Data and Method 57

similarly calculated and summed to an aggregate rate of 6.857. This aggregate rate was then multiplied by an assessment/sales price ratio of .28 and an industrial equalization factor of 1.02, for an overall effective tax rate of 1.96.

Site Quality
Municipal Capital Expenditures *(CAPOUT82)*
Capital outlays from the 1982 Survey of Government Finances, standardized by municipal land area (SQKILM), was used as an estimate of site quality. This measure includes spending on infrastructure and other capital improvements. We may speculate that firms will seek out locations where cities spend relatively more on such improvements.

Labor Force
All labor force variables are taken from the 1980 Census (Census of Population and Housing 1980). These variables are calculated for "home city plus 5-mile surrounding cities" (hereafter called "nearby") as discussed above. The point here was to choose labor force variables which would was to select measures of *potential* labor supply, and to avoid measures that indicated the *consequences* of development. For example, in trying to develop measures of available nearby labor it is necessary to avoid such variables as "workers who commute less than 20 minutes" because commute times are more a *consequence* of nearby development than a measure of potential labor. Instead, worker characteristics are better measured with variables such as household income (discussed above) and labor characteristics such as gender, race, and skill levels (discussed below).

The labor force measures used here were calculated with land area as the denominator so that the measures are density measures and not absolute numbers or "percent-of-population" based variables. Using density measures allows us to distinguish between small and large populations and to correct for the inexactness of the coding of 5-mile surrounding cities. For example, compare a town such as Woodstock, population 14,300 and land area 7.5 square miles; to Wheeling, population 29,900 with similar land area at 7.8 square miles. If both Woodstock and Wheeling each have 10,000 high school graduates within their populations, the percent-of-population value would be 70% for Woodstock and 33% for Wheeling. To use percentages would incorrectly measure "more" high school graduates in Woodstock than in Wheeling. It would be more accurate to use the absolute value of 10,000.

In addition, as discussed above, the labor force variables are measured not just for the city itself (Woodstock or Wheeling) but also for all surrounding cities within five miles. The best measure in this case is the absolute value of high school graduates in this larger area. Yet the process of hand coding surrounding cities produced inaccuracies that preclude the use of this larger-area absolute value in and of itself. As mentioned, the coding was imprecise in that we designated a city as "surrounding" if *any* portion was within the circumference of the 5-mile circle. The consequence of this was that the total *area* coded as "surrounding" differs by city, depending on the size of surrounding cities and the presence of unincorporated areas. If only the portion inside the 5-mile circle was included, the area would be about 78.5 square miles (using the formula for the area of a circle). Yet the actual area coded ranges from a low of 1.20 for the village of Peotone (surrounded by unincorporated area) to a high of 135.03 for the village of Hazel Crest (in a dense area with many cities located just at its 5-mile rim). Standardizing the labor force variables by land area corrects for this discrepancy.

Gender (*FEM_DEN* and *MEN_DEN*)
This variable uses "nearby cities" discussed above to define "the density of women of with 2 or more children under 18" (from table 57 in the 1980 Census of Population and Housing). The variable FEM_DEN is measured as (females over 15 with children 0 to 17 in nearby cities)/(total land area in 5-mile surrounding cities). Given the discussion above, we may expect that branch operations will seek out locations where the density of such women is higher.

In addition, MEN_DEN is defined as the density of men between 18 and 44 (prime working-age men). MEN_DEN is used to measure whether firms are locating in search of a *general* labor-force-aged population, or if it is women workers in particular.

College Graduates (*COL_DEN*)
COL_DEN is a measure of college graduates per square mile (1980 Census table 50), capturing the overall education level of the population. Are companies looking for well-educated labor? Perhaps not all kinds of

Data and Method

business, but it may be that this variable will be more important for business service firms than for manufacturing firms.

Elementary School Graduates (*ELEM_DEN*)
ELEM_DEN is a measure of elementary school graduates per square mile (1980 Census table 50), net of college and high school graduates, capturing populations with lower overall education levels. The reverse of COL_DEN might be true here, where manufacturing firms will seek out these populations rather than college graduate populations as would business services employers.

THE SURVEY

In addition to the statistical model outlined above, a survey was administered in order to allow companies to articulate what they believe were the considerations they took into account when choosing their current location. The rest of this chapter explains this survey--how it was designed, how it was administered and who responded.

Developing the Survey Instrument

The survey was developed with reference to questions explored in previous survey research and included: (1) questions about the company's current location, line of business, and reasons for choosing the Chicago area overall; (2) a list of factors from which firms were to choose those that affected their choice of the suburbs in general and the city in particular, and (3) a "fill-in-the-blank" matrix in which respondents were asked to characterize the occupational and gender breakdown of their current labor force. The survey was subject to the usual pre-tests and revisions.

Survey Administration

Surveys were sent to a random sample of 334 firms from the universe of 1302.[6] The mailing and follow-up procedures described below followed standard practice as discussed by Dillman (1978), including one initial and two subsequent mailings per firm, and a final fourth call in which the goal was to complete the survey over the telephone (table 5). These steps

Table 5
Disposition of Surveys

	N	Returned After 1st attempt % of N	Total Returned % of N
Pre-call	190	40.5% (77)	79.5% (151)
No pre-call	144	19.4 (28)	45.1 (66)
Total	334	31.4 (105)	65.0 (217)

produced 217 responses from this sample of 334 firms (a 65% response rate), and represented 85 of the 105 cities in the study identified as containing as least one branch firm. Sixty-three of the 217 firms did not respond while 54 companies were found to have either moved or closed doors.

A side note. One hundred ninety of these 334 firms were contacted in the weeks proceeding the first mailing to let them know that a survey would be arriving in the mail. This was a small exercise to determine whether such a pre-call would affect the response rate. The variation in response rates suggests that a pre-call does much to boost the response rate (table 5). Seventy-seven of the called sample of 190 (40.5%) responded to the questionnaire after the first attempt, while only 19.4% of the uncalled sample did so. (A test for significance between two proportions gives a value of 4.39—clearly significant at the .01 level.)

The make-up of the firms who returned surveys is not all that different from the general sample. The sample, as a reflection of the general population of firms, contained more manufactuirng than service businesses, (63% of the sample and population are manufacturing firms). Only a slightly higher percentage of service than manufacturing firms returned surveys (table 6 below), so that of the final 217 returned surveys, 59% are manufacturing firms. Firms responding to the survey encompass a broad range of industries in both the manufacturing and service sectors.

Table 6
Sample and Returns by Industry

SIC		Sample		Return %	
		Firms	Emp	Firms	Emp
20	Food Processing	16	3,767	50.0%	47.6%
22	Textile Products	2	70	50.0	71.4
23	Apparel	1	300	100.0	100.0
24	Lumber	2	78	50.0	35.9
25	Furniture	4	150	50.0	51.3
26	Paper and allied	11	928	54.6	65.3
27	Printing and publishing	11	941	45.5	55.9
28	Chemicals	31	4,877	71.0	66.1
29	Petroleum	1	279	100.0	100.0
30	Rubber	14	1,265	64.3	64.9
32	Stone, clay, glass	7	603	85.7	74.2
33	Primary metal	12	2,694	50.0	31.8
34	Fabricated metal	20	1,543	50.0	31.8
35	Industrial machinery	36	25,637	75.0	81.0
36	Electrical equipment	18	2,951	55.6	68.2
37	Transportation equip.	5	897	60.0	65.5
38	Instruments	12	1,632	50.0	71.8
39	Misc. mfg	7	406	71.4	81.6
	Manufacturing total	211	30,937	61.1	68.9
732	Credit reporting	2	350	50.0	14.3
733	Mailing	3	170	66.7	82.6
734	Services to buildings	2	40	100.0	100.0
735	Eequipment rental	9	604	55.6	68.7
736	Personnel supply	3	140	33.3	14.3
737	Computer services	19	1,494	57.9	65.5
738	Misc. business services	27	2,349	59.3	54.9
871	Engineering	17	2,065	88.2	89.2
872	Accounting	12	63	100.0	100.0
873	Research	12	771	83.3	69.0
874	Management	27	2,753	81.5	91.6
	Services total	123	10,765	71.5	73.1
Total		334	41,036	65.0	71.2

The analysis presented in the next chapter is based on these 217 responding firms. The distribution of these businesses among cities in our suburbs is similar to the distribution of the sample (compare 4 to table 7, below), again indicating that those who returned surveys are not altogether different from those whch did not. (Table 7 gives means and standard deviations for variables that appear in the statistical model for all firms, so cities may be repeated. That is, if two firms are in city "A" then the value of the variable for city "A" is counted twice.) Firms in the sample were in cities with an average of 22.48 firms, for about 3,292 employees; firms which returned the survey were in cities with an average of 22.37 firms and 3,322 employees. These "cities of responding firms" were, on average, about nine square miles, and had an average population of about 30,000. About 59% of them had direct access to a highway (since HGHWAY1 is either a "0" or a "1," the average is the percent that is "1"), and that were about 27 miles from downtown Chicago.

A Note Regarding Contact Person

One of the major difficulties with surveys regarding location decisions is that the person or persons involved with making the decision cannot always be clearly identified (Schmenner 1982). To assess the extent of this problem in this study, the survey asked whether the person filling out the questionnaire had been involved in the selection process. One-third of the respondents indicated that they had been involved. In addition, in response to the questions whether the respondent was the person to whom the questionnaire had been addressed, 80% of the returns indicated that this was the case. The surveys were invariably sent to the president, CEO, or branch manager. It is reasonable to assume that a person in such a position, even if not involved in the original decision and thus without firsthand knowledge of the original concerns, would have a sense of what is important to the firm's continued operation at the present location.

Table 7
City Variables
For Sampled and Responding Firms

Variable	Sample (N = 334)*		Returns (N=217)*	
	Mean	Standard Deviation	Mean	Standard Deviation
NUM	22.48	17.07	22.37	17.30
EMP	3291.85	2734.15	3321.98	2804.41
BSRVNUM	8.85	9.59	8.77	9.54
BSRVEMP	1100.81	1803.58	1143.29	1924.33
MFGNUM	13.65	11.08	13.62	11.14
MFGEMP	2191.06	2143.57	2178.70	2150.33
SQKILM	8.89	5.63	9.01	5.88
CPOP1000	29.72	20.65	29.30	20.88
HGHWAY1	.57	.50	.59	.49
HGHWAY2	.13	.34	.12	.33
HGHWAY3	.06	.24	.06	.25
OHARE1	.18	.38	.19	.39
OHARE2	.30	.46	.29	.45
TOLOOP	26.97	12.59	26.97	12.59
CITYAGE	84.40	29.61	85.42	29.98
CPBLACK	3.91	10.48	3.82	8.94
STOTDEN8	463.50	710.61	597.64	726.74
SMFGDEN8	482.49	320.94	499.35	321.74
MHSINC	26.10	6.94	25.92	6.94
MUNI81	1.03	.66	1.04	.67
EFRATE81	3.48	1.46	3.43	1.49
CAPOUT	82183.29	222.39	82182.51	220.10
FEM_DEN	730.31	197.60	725.88	202.36
COL_DEN	312.61	132.66	310.90	134.13
ELEM_DEN	536.37	261.81	544.74	268.59

*EFRATE81 is available for 269 sample firms and 173 responding firms.
CAPOUT82 is available for 265 sample firms and 168 responding firms.

NOTES

1. Due to the way branch listings were selected by computer from the master Dun and Bradstreet file, several suburban cities located near Chicago were not included in the list of cities. In short, listings were pulled using the county and zip code fields. City of Chicago zip codes all have the prefix 606, so the program to subset the data selected all *non* 606 prefix. Unfortunately that meant that eight cities bordering Chicago, which also have zip codes which begin with 606, were not included. These cities are Calumet Park, Cicero, Elmwood Park, Evergreen Park, Lincolnwood, Niles, Norridge, and Riverdale.

2. Firm listings differ on two dimensions: comprehensiveness and accuracy. Although a business database may be comprehensive in that it contains all of the businesses in an area of interest, it may have inaccuracies: firms no longer in business, duplicate listings, etc. It is not always possible to know which records are true and which are not. This article reveals that about 1/3 of Dun and Bradstreet records are erroneous, although it was the most comprehensive.

3. Of course, inasmuch as median commute differs by occupation, and the mix of occupations varies by industry, this median is merely an approximation for any one industry.

4. These data and some others indicated below were acquired through efforts by the Federal Reserve Bank of Chicago.

5. Land estimates were also prepared by the Federal Reserve Bank of Chicago.

6. The survey was originally sent in September, 1992, with timely follow-up.

IV
The Evidence: Determinants of Firm Location

Here we discuss what the survey and the statistical model can tell us about the relative importance of the factors discussed in previous chapters, especially the role of workers, to the firm location decision. The first sections present findings from the statistical model and highlight some of these findings with results from the survey, by discussing each variable or specific characteristic separately. Then, the survey results themselves are summarized, with particular attention to the role of workers. Finally, we compare the two methods. The survey is used to inquire into the accuracy of the statistical measures, and conversely, the statistical measures are used to further investigate the meaning behind survey responses.

WHAT DOES THE MODEL TELL US?

The numbers from the statistical model tell us that most standard factors are important to firms: access to the highway, inexpensive land, etc., and that labor force factors do play a role in enitcing firms to cities in the suburbs (the output from the statistical model for "locations," meaning number of firms, and employment are presented in table 8; correlations among variables can be found in table 9). The discussion of the coefficients in the following sections focuses on the relative importance and direction of each measure in the model.

City Size and Site Availability

As expected from the previous discussion, both manufacturing and business services firms seek out cities with higher populations (the coefficient on CPOP1000 is positive and significant), but as the population density of both the city and surrounding area grows, companies find other locations (the coefficient on POP_DEN is negative, see table 8). Thus, higher densities drive out industrial and commercial uses. More persons per square mile indicates less land available for development, more competition for land and thus higher prices, and more congestion and other urban deterrents. These obstacles seem somewhat more important for manufacturing than for business services firms. Higher population density seems to mean fewer and smaller manufacturers, but only seems to affect the size (not the number) of businesses services firms. We may interpret this to mean that business services firms find a way to "squeeze in" in crowded cities, but are not large firms, while manufacturing firms avoid these cities altogether.

This is supported by the survey responses. Although the survey did not, obviously, ask the companies "did you avoid cities with high population densities?" it did ask about the importance of land costs (Q9B) and available land (Q8G). (A copy of the survey form can be found in appendix 2). Both "land costs" and "lots of available land" were chosen by a larger percentage of manufacturing firms than of business services firms (27% of business services firms chose "land costs," while 47% of manufacturers did so; for "lots of available land" the proportions were 24% and 38% respectively). And it was the larger firms in both sectors that were concerned with these factors. The average size of a manufacturing firm which checked the box for "land costs" on the survey was 201 employees, while the average size for those that did not was 128; the average size of a business services firm which chose "land costs" was 161, for those that did not it was 62. Similar proportions hold for "lots of available land."

In addition, firms which indicated on the survey that they were concerned about finding *available* land tended to go to cities with lower population densities. (See the section "Comparing Survey Answers to Municipal Measures," and table 17, below). However, density did not seem to matter to firms looking for *low-cost* land, suggesting that density measures are better seen as substitute measures for "land availability" than for "land costs."

Table 8
Regression Coefficients—203 Suburban Cities

Independent Variable	Total Firms	Total Emp	Manufacturing Firms	Manufacturing Emp	Business Services Firms	Business Services Emp
CPOP1000	.043	.069	.035	.058	.055	.112
	(.007)*	(.017)*	(.008)*	(.017)*	(.007)	(.018)*
POP_DEN	-2.102	-4.443	-2.037	-4.269	-1.099	-2.087
	(.589)*	(1.308)*	(.596)*	(1.349)*	(.558)	(1.394)
HGHWAY1	.643	1.047	.644	1.409	.665	1.051
	(.284)*	(.631)*	(.288)*	(.651)*	(.269)*	(.673)
HGHWAY2	-.026	-.408	-.029	-.068	.577	.898
	(.357)	(.793)	(.362)	(.818)	(.338)*	(.845)
HGHWAY3	-.371	-1.065	-.272	-.718	.164	.092
	(.319)	(.709)	(.323)	(.732)	(.302)	(.755)
OHARE1	1.740	1.543	1.114	.737	2.259	3.584
	(.691)*	(1.534)	(.699)	(1.582)	(.654)*	(1.634)*
OHARE2	.571	.517	.465	.725	1.026	1.757
	(.350)*	(.784)	(.357)	(.809)	(.334)*	(.836)*
STOTDEN8	.0007	.0015	.0008	.002	.0002	.0003
	(.0003)*	(.0007)*	(.0003)*	(.001)*	(.0003)	(.0007)
CPBLACK	-.002	-.012	.003	.002	-.0006	-.007
	(.007)	(.015)	(.007)	(.016)	(.006)	(.016)
MHSINC	-.012	-.031	-.026	-.063	.029	.065
	(.012)	(.028)	(.01)*	(.029)*	(.012)*	(.030)*
CITYAGE	.027	.059	.029	.061	.008	.017
	(.004)*	(.009)*	(.004)*	(.009)*	(.004)*	(.009)*
MUNI81	-.408	-.591	-.513	-.831	-.164	-.187
	(.197)*	(.437)	(.199)*	(.451)*	(.186)	(.465)
FEM_DEN	.006	.014	.005	.010	.005	.009
	(.003)*	(.006)*	(.003)*	(.007)	(.003)*	(.007)
MEN_DEN	.002	.005	.002	.005	-.0004	-.0003
	(.002)	(.005)	(.002)	(.005)	(.002)	(.005)
COL_DEN	.188	.4186	.191	.432	.178	.446
	(.830)	(.844)	(.409)	(.903)	(.786)	(.965)

Table 8 continued on next page

Table 8 continued

Independent Variable	Total		Manufacturing		Business Services	
	Firms	Emp	Firms	Emp	Firms	Emp
CONSTANT	-1.484	-.419	-1.072	.949	-2.980	-3.805
	(.629)*	(1.400)	(.637)	(1.442)	(.596)*	(1.489)*
R^2	.529	.448	.487	.429	.491	.376
Adjusted R^2	.494	.407	.448	.387	.453	.329

*Significant at the .1 level

What is not entered in the model in this category ("city size and site availability") from the possible variables mentioned in chapter 3 is the size of the city in square kilometers (SQKILM). Investigation of the correlation matrix (table 9) revealed that land area (SQKILM) and population (CPOP1000) were highly correlated, and so both could not be entered in the model.[1]

Transportation Access

Access to highway entrance and exit ramps (HGHWAY1) is important for the location and size of manufacturing firms and for the site of (but not for the employment levels of) business services firms. This is to be expected, taking into account the fact that manufacturers are concerned with truck and other large-vehicle traffic, and the amount of such traffic most likely varies by firm size. Yet having a highway accessible with 2 miles (HGHWAY2) or within 5 miles (HGHWAY3) does not correspond with more branch company locations. It seems as though companies needing highway access desire *direct* access to an exit/entrance ramp--being close is not good enough. The further a business is located from a ramp, the more viaducts, narrow roads, and other truck barriers will come into play.

Again, survey responses shed light on these findings. What is at first puzzling is that of those firms responding to the survey, a larger proportion of *business services firms* than of manufacturing companies indicated that they chose their location to be near highways (66% vs. 53%). However, it was *smaller* firms on average in business services that said "yes" to the highway factor, while in the manufacturing sector it was *larger* firms. This explains why in the model highway access was related to manufacturing

Table 9
Correlation Coefficients

Variable	SQKILM	CPOP1000	POP_DEN	HGHWY1	HGHWY2	HGHWY3	OHARE1	OHARE2	TOLOOP	CITYAGE	CPBLACK
SQKILM	1.00										
CPOP1000	.76*	1.00									
POP_DEN	-.39*	.04	1.00								
HGHWY1	.21	.26*	.20	1.00							
HGHWY2	-.15	-.06	.22	-.35*	1.00						
HGHWY3	-.17	-.07	.10	-.38*	-.15	1.00					
OHARE1	.02	-.02	.12	.06	.20	-.09	1.00				
OHARE2	-.06	.10	.40*	.11	.03	-.14	-.15	1.00			
TOLOOP	.37*	.01	-.74*	-.20	-.18	-.05	-.13	-.33*	1.00		
CITYAGE	.29*	.26*	-.02	-.05	.00	-.10	.03	-.05	.06	1.00	
CPBLACK	-.02	.15	.21	.13	.01	-.06	-.09	-.03	.08	.13	1.00
MHSINC	-.19	-.13	-.18	.02	-.15	.05	-.08	-.04	-.13	.04	-.35*
MUNI81	.01	.33*	.46*	.15	.04	.01	-.18	.06	-.26*	.34*	.60*
EFRATE81	-.37*	.00	.67*	.22	.05	.12	-.07	.10	-.54*	-.07	.32*
CAPOUT82	-.06	.31*	.19	-.09	.05	.11	-.05	.15	-.16	.20	.27*
FEM_DEN	-.37*	.04	.63*	.17	.23	.11	.12	.34*	-.50*	-.12	.19
MEN_DEN	-.33*	.09	.66*	.17	.23	.09	.12	.30*	-.46*	-.11	.22
ELEM_DEN	-.39*	-.04	.74*	.18	.27*	.05	.10	.23	-.37*	.02	.28*
COL_DEN	-.12	.17	.55*	.13	-.03	.06	.09	.27*	-.38*	.12	-.02
STOTDEN8	-.31*	.03	.47*	.19	.22	.00	.33*	.50*	-.47*	.12	.07
SMFGDEN8	-.28*	-.02	.35*	.17	.27*	-.07	.39*	.46*	-.52*	.12	.08

Table 9 continued on next page

Table 9 continued

Variable	MHSINC	MUNI81	EFRATE81	CAPOUT82	FEM_DEN	MEN_DEN	ELEM_DEN	COL_DEN	STOTDEN8	SMFGDEN8
SQKILM										
CPOP1000										
POP_DEN										
HGHWY1										
HGHWY2										
HGHWY3										
OHARE1										
OHARE2										
TOLOOP										
CITYAGE										
CPBLACK										
MHSINC	1.00									
MUNI81	-.21	1.00								
EFRATE81	-.06	.53*	1.00							
CAPOUT82	-.17	.32*	.09	1.00						
FEM_DEN	-.18	.41*	.53*	.19	1.00					
MEN_DEN	-.25*	.39*	.47*	.20	.68	1.00				
ELEM_DEN	-.40*	.49*	.51*	.11	.63*	.57*	1.00			
COL_DEN	.36*	.23	.30*	.30*	.32*	.38*	.15	1.00		
STOTDEN8	-.11	.35*	.43*	.23	.53*	.51*	.47*	.43*	1.00	
SMFGDEN8	-.21	.29*	.32*	.19	.40*	.40*	.44*	.34*	.95	1.00

* Significant at the .05 Level

Determinants of Firm Location

employment but not to business services employment. The implication of this is that the reasons for desiring highway access may differ between sectors. Large manufacturers may want to be near highways in order to facilitate freight traffic, while business services locate near highways for visibility or for access to the large manufacturing firms.

Proximity to the airport (OHARE1 and OHARE2) matters for the location and size of business services, but not for manufacturing, branches. The speculation that this variable in the statistical model would capture the dampening effect of airport proximity on residential land uses and land prices seems not to be the case. If it were the case, manufacturing firms would choose locations near the airport at least as much, if not more so, than business services. But in fact, survey findings support the model estimates—55% of business services firms responded that proximity to O'Hare was important, while only 24% of manufacturing firms did so. In addition, firms which said they were concerned with land costs were no more likely to locate in cities near the airport than businesses which were not so concerned (table 17). This evidence suggests that proximity to O'Hare does not mean lower land costs, in perception if not in fact, to firms.

There seems to be a tradeoff, however, between proximity to O'Hare and available land. This tradeoff may help explain why the the statistical model found significant "O'Hare" coefficients for business services but not manufacturing. Companies concerned about available land tended to go to cities farther from both the airport and from highways (table 17). Given that in the survey it was manufacturers who were more likely to give land availability high priority (discussed above), it may be that for manufacturers, land availability is more important than being near airports, when the choice has to be made.

Distance to the Loop (TOLOOP), not included in this final model, was highly correlated with employment and population densities (table 9). "Distance to the Loop" was meant to capture the effects of land prices, and the proximity to potential suppliers and buyers. However, the discussion of survey results below suggest that these concepts are captured by median household incomes, the density of surrounding employment, and population density (table 17 below).

City Characteristics

The coefficients for African-American populations are not significant (CPBLACK). This finding is unexpected and survey answers suggest why. Firms which on the survey answered that they were looking for low-wage labor, or labor in general went to suburban cities with higher black populations than those that were not looking for such labor (table 17). Perhaps, in the model, the behavior of these firms "cancelled out" the effect of firms that avoid minority populations for the reasons discussed above (real or perceived crime rates, disinvestment, etc). This is supported by the fact that firms which chose the suburbs for quality of life considerations chose areas with fewer minorities (table 17).

Higher median household incomes (MHSINC) are associated with less manufacturing activity yet more locations and employment in business services. Higher income communities are more likely than are lower income to zone out objectionable kinds of development (manufacturing land uses), while business services may be more acceptable. What may also be part of the effect here is that business services are more likely to have need for high-end labor and such labor is more likely to come from higher-income communities. In fact, establishments worried about labor costs went to areas with lower median incomes (table 17).

The age of a city (CITYAGE) is associated with more manufacturing firms and employment and more business services locations. This supports the contention that older cities are more likely to have a history of industrial activity than are newer and thus be more amenable to manufacturing development, in the form of appropriate zoning, available buildings and industrial sites. Yet what is also revealed here is that this industrial history may also make the community attractive to the location (if not the size of) business services firms, perhaps for the same reasons or perhaps because business services locate in order to be near other firms. Comparing survey responses to the municipal database suggests that firms locating to such older towns are looking for low-cost labor and suppliers (table 17).

Proximity to Other Businesses

The density of surrounding employment was designed to capture the effects of supplier and customer linkages for firms. Two measures capturing this notion were available--the density of surrounding *total* employment

Determinants of Firm Location

(STOTDEN8) and the density of surrounding *manufacturing* employment (SMFGDEN8) were correlated at the .95 level. Total employment was chosen because it was thought to be a better measure in terms of capturing output linkages for business services (they supply not just manufacturing but all industries). Yet the results show that proximity to other businesses was important to manufacturing firms but not to business services (calculating the equations with SMFGDEN8 did not change this discrepancy).

The survey suggests that the model results here may be inconclusive because of the need to assess input and output linkages separately. Business services are much more likely to be concerned about being close to customers (43% of business services) than about being close to suppliers (5%), while manufacturers were concerned about both roughly equally (20% said close to suppliers while 28% said close to customers). Comparing survey answers to the municipal database suggests that the density of surrounding employment is a better measure of supplier linkages than customer linkages (table 17), so that the model may be measuring the effects of supplier proximity (more important to manufacturers than business services). This may explain why the coefficients are significant for manufacturers but not for business services. If separate measures for suppliers and for markets were available, the coefficients for markets in the business services equations may be significant.

Tax Rate

The tax rate available for the full set of 203 cities was the municipal tax rate (MUNI81). Municipal tax rates have a negative influence on manufacturing firm locations, but not size, and not business services. The same findings hold below, where for cities of 10,000 and greater population a separate equation was run using effective tax rates in place of municipal tax rates.

The survey did not ask specifically about tax rates, but these branch firms did have the opportunity to mention tax rates in the open-ended questions asking about other reasons for choosing the suburbs or a particular city in the suburbs. Five of the 217 firms did so: three of these were manufacturers and two were business services. What is interesting is that it does not seem as though these firms were aggressive about searching out the lowest rates available: of these five, three chose cities where the tax rate (municipa ratel, or effective rate when available) was *higher* than the average for all cities.

Labor Force

Other studies of company locations, as discussed in previous chapters, suggest that the availability of second-earner women, women with family responsibilities, entices firms to the suburbs and to particular suburbs. Here, the measure which attempts to measure the presence of these women is FEM_DEN, the density of women of any age with children under 17. What we find is that FEM_DEN influences the number of firm locations, but not the employment in, both manufacturing and business services firms. The fact that the model also controls for the density of men aged 18-44 (MEN_DEN, which is not significant) implies that the significance of FEM_DEN is not just capturing the effects of the availability of a labor-force-aged population, but specifically of women with household responsibilities.[2] Interpretation of the survey results with respect to female labor force is treated at length in the section "Female Labor" below. What is most of note from that section is that firms who chose the suburbs looking for low-cost labor went to areas with a higher density of women with children (table 17).

However, education levels (COL_DEN) of the population do not seem to affect the location or employment levels of firms. It could be that this variable is not a fine enough measure of labor skills to capture the effects of labor pools of particular skills. As suggested by Hanson and Pratt (1992) firms are often looking for very specific labor skills.

Fit and Limitations of the Model

Overall, the model gives a better fit when predicting manufacturing and business services together than when estimating either sector separately (by comparing the size of the R^2 in table 8). This could be an artifact of statistical modeling whereby a model captures the average behavior of a group better than the behavior of any one subset. This suggests that the model does not adequately identify the variables important to each group separately; perhaps zoning, city policies, the presence of customers and suppliers as suggested by the disscussion above, etc.

In addition, when estimating each separately, it does a better job at manufacturing than business services. It may be that the factors which influence manufacturing locations are more amenable to the constraints of statistical modeling which requires all variables to be quantifiable: distance to highways, age of cities, etc.; while the reasons business services firms

Determinants of Firm Location 75

choose cities are more disparate and qualitative: quality of life, friendly city government, etc. What is also possible is that we know less about what is important to business services firms and the model does not contain the factors important to these firms.

What is evident from survey responses is that a few of the factors chosen more often by business services than manufacturing firms are also more qualitative in nature and so less suitable to statistical modeling. Specifically, business services firms were concerned with the availability of quality, inexpensive office space and with choosing a site with a good "image". The importance of these factors are revealed by both the close- and open-ended questions. As mentioned above, business services companies were more likely to choose "good building available" from the given list than were manufacturers. On the open-ended questions, business services branches gave answers such as "lower rent," "image," "high tech area," and "newer building." No manufacturers mentioned rent or building factors specifically, but gave answers such as "access to water and railways" (which perhaps should have been included in the model).

The model also gives a better prediction for locations (numbers of firms) than for employment levels. This can be explained in that the independent variables are municipal level variables which specifically affect the choice of a particular city for a firm, but not necessarily the choice of an employment size. Branch employment within cities is dependent on the number of firms located within municipal boundaries, but also depends on the size of the firms. Firm size could perhaps be better predicted by several municipal variables that this model lacks: zoning regulations, measures of vacant land, etc.; but is also influenced by internal decisions not subject to statistical modeling.

Cities for which the model significantly under- or over-predicted branch activity are shown in table 10. (Significant residuals were defined as a studentized residual greater than 1.96, or two standard deviations.) Among those places consistently over-predicted (where the model suggested that there should be more activity than there really is) are cities which are primarily residential in character (Hanover Park, Highwood, Lake Villa, Glen Ellyn, Western Springs), and where a large percent of the land is Forest Preserve, cemetery or park land (Justice, Crete). This suggests that the model could be improved by incorporating zoning or land use variables. In these places, it was manufacturing specifically that was over-predicted. In

Table 10
Significant* Studentized Residual Terms by Dependent Variable

City	Total Num	Total Emp	Manufacturing Num	Manufacturing Emp	Business Services Num	Business Services Emp
Hanover Park	-2.31	-2.32				
Highwood	-2.29	-2.36	-2.32	-2.35		
Brookfield	-2.29	-2.28				
Justice	2.14	-2.22	-1.97	-2.04		
Crete		-2.12				
Lake Villa		-2.02				
Glen Ellyn			-2.85	-2.63		
Berwyn			-2.67	-2.52		
Rosemont			-2.29			
Oak Lawn			-2.57	-2.08		
Western Springs			-2.18	-2.29		
Park Forest	2.24	2.19	2.25	2.40		
Oak Brook	3.02	2.17	2.19	2.07	2.70	
Bridgeview	2.11		2.35			
Lisle	2.15		2.01		2.05	
Countryside	2.17		1.98			
Warrenville		1.97				
Westmont					2.31	
Hinsdale					2.00	
Round Lake						2.91
Batavia						2.12
Worth						2.09
Crestwood						2.03

*Significant is defined as higher than two standard deviations.

fact, the model did not significantly over-predict business services in any municipality.

Considering those places which were under-predicted (that is, the model thought that there should be less branch activity in that city than there actually is), there occurs a set of cities where the model under-predicted the numbers of branch firms locating in the city but not branch employment, suggesting that these cities host a large number of small firms (Bridgeview, Lisle and Countryside). Bridgeview and Countryside share the characteristic

Determinants of Firm Location

of bordering the principal Chicago railroad freight yards in Bedford Park, indicating that the model could benefit from the addition of a "proximity to railroad" variable. Park Forest and Oak Brook are consistently under-predicted for both total and manufacturing activity. In the case of Park Forest, the underlying data reveals that the under-prediction seems to be the result of one relatively large company in a relatively small town.

Reduced Form Equation

In order to check whether the statistical model actually is a "good fit," it is common practice to also estimate a "reduced form equation," where all the insignificant variables are removed the equation is re-estimated. This reduced form of the equation is given in table 11. All variables identified as significant in the original equation remain so, attesting to the robustness of the original estimation.

Evidence for Cities of 10,000 and Greater Population

Variables which may better measure true municipal conditions were available for 98 cities which had 1980 populations of 10,000 and over.[3] These two measures are EFATE81 (effective tax rates in 1981) and CAPOUT82 (municipal capital expenditures outlays per square kilometer). Capital outlays are a measure of how much a municipality may spend on infrastructure improvements such as roads, sewers, bridges, and the like.

What is immediately apparent from table 12 is that population density (POP_DEN) and the density of women with children (FEM_DEN) are no longer significant when considering just this subset of places (table 12 takes just the significant variables from table 9 above and adds EFRATE81 and CAPOUT82). What this may suggest is that at a certain population level a threshold is achieved in terms of population density and worker availability, and companies are then indifferent among places.

It also seems that "effective tax rate" is a better predictor of industrial location than is just the municipal tax rate. (The model for the 203 cities discussed above found municipal rates significant only for manufacturing activity, while in the model here for 98 cities the effective tax rate is associated with both manufacturing and business services). We expect this, given that the two measures were not highly correlated (.25) and given that effective tax rates are a closer measure of the tax bill faced by firms.

Table 11
Reduced Form Regression Coefficients—203 Suburban Cities

Independent Variable	Total		Manufacturing		Business Services	
	Firms	Emp	Firms	Emp	Firms	Emp
CPOP1000	.046	.069	.038	.076	.053	.119
	(.007)*	(.016)*	(.007)*	(.016)*	(.007)*	(.015)*
POP_DEN	-2.072	-5.395	-2.261	-1.340	-.97	
	(.570)*	(1.196)*	(.549)*	(.320)*	(.468)*	
HGHWAY1	.738	1.469	.777	1.412	.595	
	(.232)*	(.518)*	(.234)*	(.525)*	(.232)*	
HGHWAY2					-.974	
					(.303)*	
OHARE1	1.912				2.563	4.296
	(.682)*				(.560)*	(1.371)*
OHARE2	.656				1.166	1.891
	(.344)				(.269)*	(.595)*
STOTDEN8	.0006	.0021	.0010	.0020		
	(.0003)*	(.0005)*	(.0002)*	(.0005)*		
MHSINC			-.032	-.078	.032	.074
			(.012)*	(.027)*	(.011)*	(.027)*
CITYAGE	.028	.058	.029	.054	.007	.009
	(.004)*	(.008)*	(.004)*	(.008)*	(.003)*	(.008)
MUNI81	-.439		-.583	-1.059		
	(.186)*		(.184)*	(.418)*		
FEM_DEN	.008	.021	.008		.004	
	(.003)*	(.006)*	(.003)*		(.002)*	
CONST.	-1.877	-1.572	-.891	2.577	-3.070	-3.789
	(.404)*	(.892)*	(.601)	(1.284)*	(.560)*	(1.074)*
Adjusted R^2	.497	.397	.450	.376	.453	.337

* Significant at the .1 level.

Finally, capital expenditures per square kilometer (CAPOUT82), which can be thought of as a measure of site quality positively influences branch activity. It seems to be more important for business services firms than manufacturers. This, coupled with the survey evidence which indicated that business services firms are concerned about available buildings while

Table 12
Regression Coefficients—Cities of 10,000 and Greater

Independent Variables	Total		Manufacturing		Business Services	
	Firms	Emp	Firms	Emp	Firms	Emp
CPOP1000	.026	.034	.021	.035	.039	.082
	(.008)*	(.018)*	(.010)*	(.021)*	(.009)*	(.021)*
POP_DEN	-.275	-1.878	-1.177	-1.461	-.441	
	(.744)	(1.450)	(.829)	(.553)*	(.666)	
HGHWAY1	.639	1.210	.705	1.342	1.077	
	(.276)*	(.580)*	(.331)*	(.697)*	(.334)*	
HGHWAY2					1.035	
					(.482)*	
OHARE1	2.448				1.705	3.001
	(.733)*				(.560)*	(1.54)*
OHARE2	1.123				.887	1.494
	(.392)*				(.361)*	(.752)*
STOTDEN8	.00008	.0015	.011	.0021		
	(.0004)	(.0006)*	(.0004)*	(.0007)*		
MHSINC			-.062	-.101	.069	.158
			(.027)*	(.057)*	(.025)*	(.060)*
CITYAGE	.015	.037	.016	.031	.003	.005
	(.005)*	(.011)*	(.006)*	(.011)*	(.006)	(.011)
FEM_DEN	.00008	.006	.002	.001		
	(.0003)	(.007)	(.004)	(.003)		
EFRATE81	-.204	-.511	-.257	-.468	-.200	-.411
	(.110)*	(.227)*	(.130)*	(.265)*	(.121)*	(.202)*
CAPOUT82	.001	.0018	.0007	.002	.001	.003
	(.0006)*	(.0013)	(.0007)	(.002)	(.0007)*	(.001)*
CONSTANT	-1.034	3.398	2.222	7.158	-2.451	-2.653
	(.754)	(1.548)*	(1.169)*	(2.22)*	(1.094)*	(2.141)
Adjusted R^2	.490	.357	.435	.322	.422	.258

*Significant at the .1 level.

manufacturing firms cared about available land, suggests that business services firms look for an available infrastructure; manufacturers may be more willing to start "from the ground up."

EVIDENCE FROM THE SURVEY

The survey evidence discussed so far was used to shed light on the regression coefficients and to suggest strengths and limitations of the model. However, the survey responses themselves can tell us much about what firms perceive to be the important factors that led them to chose and remain in a suburban location. This section now focuses solely on the survey findings themselves. First, the overall survey responses are discussed and then a section is devoted just to the evidence for women workers.

Firms were asked general questions about their organization and the make-up of their workforce, and were also given a list of factors that they may have taken into account when making their location decision. The survey asked firms both about "why did you choose the suburbs in general?" and "why did you choose this *particular* suburb?" decisions (see appendix 2 for the survey questionnaire). They were given the option of circling as many factors as applied to their situation, and were not asked to rank factors. The percent of firms which indicated the factor influenced their choice of site is given in table 13.

Originations - Where Did the Firms Come From?

Question six on the survey questionnaire asked was this a relocation or a new facility?" For branches which indicated they moved to their current location from somewhere else (a relocation), questions six and seven then allow us to distinguish five types of moves: those that moved from site to site within the same city; companies which moved from another suburb to the current suburb; those that moved out from the city of Chicago; firms that moved from another city in Illinois; and those that relocated from out-of-state. The majority of originations were inter-suburban moves. Thirty-one percent of those responding indicated that their move had been from another suburb, while another 6% had relocated from within the same city. This indicates that for the majority of firms the last relocation was a "second-stage" decision (choosing a particular city or site), so that the survey question regarding the second-stage decision ("why did you choose this particular suburb?") may be of the most importance. This also suggests that the competition for economic development activity that suburban cities face comes from other nearby suburbs, rather than from the central city. They lose

Table 13
Companies Which Checked "Yes, Factor was Important" by Industry Type

Question		Total #	Total %	Manufacturing #	Manufacturing %	Bsnss Services #	Bsnss Services %
Suburban Choice							
Q8A	Quality of life	76	35.0	43	33.6	33	37.5
Q8B	Otheer branch close	19	8.7	14	10.9	5	5.7
Q8C	Labor skills	76	35.0	41	32.0	35	39.8
Q8D	Female labor	18	8.3	10	7.8	8	9.1
Q8E	Available labor	83	38.2	54	42.2	29	33.0
Q8F	Labor costs	51	23.5	34	26.6	17	19.3
Q8G	Available land	70	32.2	49	38.3	21	23.9
City Choice							
Q9A	Labor costs	59	27.2	43	33.9	16	18.2
Q9B	Land costs	84	38.7	60	47.2	24	27.3
Q9C	Good building	102	47.0	52	40.9	50	56.8
Q9D	Airport	78	35.9	30	23.6	48	54.5
Q9E	Highway	125	57.6	67	52.8	58	65.9
Q9F	Headquarters close	16	7.4	10	7.9	6	6.8
Q9G	Other branch close	21	9.7	12	9.4	9	10.2
Q9H	Suppliers	30	13.8	26	20.5	4	4.5
Q9I	Customers	74	34.1	36	28.3	38	43.2
Q9J	Owner's home close	43	19.8	25	19.7	18	20.5
Q9K	City subsidy	12	5.5	10	7.9	2	2.3
Q9L	Quality of life	59	27.2	37	29.1	22	25.0
Q9M	Friendly government	24	11.1	20	15.9	4	4.5
Total (n)*		217		129		88	

*Columns do not round to total because firms could check more than one response.

firms to nearby cities, but by the same token they may also lure firms from other cities nearby.

Reasons for Choosing the Suburbs

Clearly, the most important factors for firms in choosing the suburbs were the availability of appropriate labor, available land, and quality of life (table13 above). All of these considerations were chosen by about one-third of responding firms. The cost of labor ranked behind availability. Except for labor skills, labor factors were chosen more often by manufacturing than by business services firms; nearly half of the manufacturers indicated that the suburban choice was concerned with labor availability, while only one-third of business service firms did so. However, business services were slightly more likely to select female labor. Just as important as labor factors were the availability of land and quality of life considerations, with land more important to manufacturing companies and quality of life chosen more often by business services.[4]

Overview of Reasons for Choosing a Particular City

Overall, the top three reasons for choosing a particular city (table 13, answers to Q9) were highway access, building availability, and land costs, indicating that the choice of a city has very much to do with specific site characteristics. Businesses chose the suburbs in general for labor and quality of life concerns, but then chose a particular city with land, building and access needs in mind. Manufacturers were more concerned with the cost of land, while business services branches looked for available buildings, suggesting that manufacturing firms are more likely to be planning to construct their own building while business services are looking for existing office space. Highway access was chosen by a larger percent of business services companies, although it was the top choice for manufacturers. As discussed above it was, on average, the smaller business services firms which chose highway access yet the larger manufacturers looked for land. Above we considered the possibility that business services and manufacturers prefer highway access for different reasons: business services for visibility, manufacturers for freight traffic.

Proximity to the airport, closeness to customers, and quality of life factors followed the top three choices. Airport access was more important to business services firms, who are more likely to need to transport people than goods. In addition, and as would be expected, proximity to customers was also chosen by a larger proportion of business services firms. Quality of life factors were chosen evenly between manufacturing and business services firms.

Factors, by Reasons for Choosing Chicago

It might be interesting to investigate how survey responses differed according to why the firm made the choice to locate in the Chicago area. For economic development planners trying to entice businesses toChicago or its suburbs, it may be of interest to know the factors contributing to making Chicago an attractive area in general for different kinds of firms. The survey offered companies four reasons for locating in the Chicago area in general (Q7).[5] Reasons for choosing the suburbs and the particular suburban city differed somewhat among the four response categories to Q7. First, firms which said that they located "in order to move out of Chicago" (i.e., they answered A to question 7) cited land availability and land costs most often as their first- and second-stage reasons, respectively. In fact, among the four categories, land considerations were chosen most often by firms leaving Chicago. It seems, therefore, that land considerations are one of the most important factors driving firms from the central city.

Second, firms which moved from somewhere else in order to be near Chicago (response B to question 7) most often chose "access to customers" as a reason for choosing the particular city. Finally, airport and highway access was most important to firms which opened a new branch near Chicago although the headquarters was located somewhere else (answer D to question 7). This suggests that when the headquarters is elsewhere, it is important for the branch firm to have good transportation access.

A Special Look at Women Workers

The presence of women workers as an important criterion in the location decision was chosen by 18 of our branch firms, or 8.3% of those responding (table 13 above). Although this was the most infrequently chosen factor in terms of the stage one decision, answers to other survey questions provides some clues as to the nature of "female branch employment" in the suburbs. First, firms which indicated the importance of female labor actually did employ more women than the metropolitan average for their 3-digit industry.[6] "Women-worker" firms employed, on average, 11 more women per firm than the average. (Non-women-worker companies employed eight fewer and the t-test for this difference is significant at the .05 level).

Second, these firms were more weighted toward business services than the sample as a whole—44% of women-worker firms were business services while only 35% of the total sample were in this sector. Answers to "could you describe what kind of work is done at this plant?" supports the notion that "female" business services branch employment in the suburbs is comprised of entry-level, back-office operations. All but one of the answers to this question indicated the work was this back-office type:[7]

1. Distribution center for health care products customer service
2. Process magazine subscriptions for libraries
3. "Paperwork" bids—order processing—no inventory
4. Telemarketing/inside sales
5. Sales office and service center
6. Disability management by RN for insurance carriers
7. Computer customer services
8. Civil engineering office

Third, the occupations in both these business services firms and in manufacturing firms tended to be less professional and technical than industry averages.[8] Women-worker firms employed about nine fewer of professional and technical occupations each, but five more clerical workers and twelve more production workers. Firms which did not choose female labor mirrored the metropolitan averages with respect to professional and technical jobs, averaged two fewer clerical, and three more production.

Fourth, not surprisingly, labor force factors in general were more important to these firms than to firms which did not check the female labor factor (table 14 below). Firms which indicated women workers were important were also much more likely to choose the other labor force factors on the survey: labor skills, labor availability and labor costs for both suburbs in general and city in particular. This suggests that for firms where women workers are important, characteristics of the labor force pool in general are central to the location decision. Other factors are about as important to these firms as to other firms. The exception seems to be that these firms are willing to trade proximity to customers for a better quality of life.

Finally, firms which were looking for women are located in the same cities as other firms. In other words, it does not seem as though firms which checked "female-labor" clustered in one or another part of the metropolitan area or chose cities not chosen by other firms.[9] In fact some women-worker firms *left* cities that were home to other women-worker branches. This all suggests that the suburbs in general may be a good location for female labor, but that other factors decide the choice among suburbs.

Determinants of Firm Location

Table 14
Frequency of Survey Responses by Q8D (Female Labor was Important)

Question		Yes	No	Total
Suburban Choice				
Q8A	Quality of life	55.9%	33.2%	35.1%
Q8B	Other branch close	6.1	8.8	8.9
Q8C	Labor skills	77.8	30.9	35.1
Q8E	Available labor	83.1	34.2	37.8
Q8F	Labor costs	44.2	22.1	23.0
Q8G	Available land	49.9	31.1	32.8
City Choices				
Q9A	Labor costs	59.1	24.9	27.2
Q9B	Land costs	46.9	38.1	38.9
Q9C	Good building	53.2	46.8	46.8
Q9D	Airport	47.1	35.1	35.9
Q9E	Highway	64.8	58.1	57.8
Q9F	Headquarters close	12.1	6.9	7.1
Q9G	Other branch close	0.0	11.2	9.9
Q9H	Suppliers	17.8	14.1	13.9
Q9I	Customers	17.9	35.9	33.9
Q9J	Owner's home close	18.1	21.9	20.1
Q9K	City subsidy	0.0	6.8	6.1
Q9L	Quality of life	41.1	18.9	26.9
Q9M	Friendly government	13.2	15.2	10.8
% Manufacturing		56	60	56
Average employment		117	136	135
Number of firms(n)		18	199	217

A second way to investigate the "women workers" question is to take a look at firms which hire more women than the metropolitan average, whether or not they explicitly indicated they were looking for female labor in the questionnaire.[10] Much of what was presented above for the firms which chose the female labor factor on the survey is also the case for this second set of firms. Again, the proportion of these firms in business services is greater than the sample as a whole: 44%, compared to 35% in the sample. In addition, on average they hire fewer professional and technical workers yet more clerical and production (for the manufacturers), while the opposite tends to be the case for firms hiring fewer women than the average for their industry in the metropolitan area. Firms with more women have an average of three more clerical jobs and eight more production, but two less professional and eight fewer technical. Branches with less women hire four more technical workers, three fewer clerical and about the average number of production workers.

Firms which hire more women are also similar to "women-worker" firms in that labor force factors in general on the survey were more important to these firms than to companies where the labor force is made up of fewer women. These firms were more likely to choose the labor force factors listed on the survey: labor skills, labor availability and labor costs for the suburbs and the city (table 15). Again, other factors are about as important to these firms as to the rest of the sample, with the exception being that these firms are willing to trade proximity to customers and suppliers for a better quality of life. Finally, as with the women-worker firms, an examination of the individual firm data indicates that there seems to be no discernable pattern with respect to city location.

COMPARING THE SURVEY TO THE DATABASE

The advantage of having information from both a survey and a statistical model is that it is possible to compare survey answers to the municipal data gathered for the equations (including measures gathered but not used in the final equations). To do this, the set of surveyed firms are divided into two groups for each factor included in the survey: firms which indicated that the factor was important, and those which did not.[11] We can then compare the means of a relevant city-level variable for the cities which said yes the factor was important ("yes" firms) to the mean of the variable for cities which did not say yes ("no" firms). For example, some firms indicated that land costs were important, while others did not. The means off variables which approximate for land costs, such as housing density, population density, and median household income can be compared for the two sets of firms.

This exercise addresses three related questions. First, it allows us to examine the extent to which measures typically included in statistical models, including the one presented here, adequately reflect the variables they were meant to represent. Statistically different means between groups

Table 15
Frequency of Survey Responses by Women Workers Employed

Question		Greater than Average	Less than Average	Total
Suburban Choice				
Q8A	Quality of life	41.9%	32.1%	35.1%
Q8B	Other branch close	9.1	9.9	8.9
Q8C	Labor skills	35.9	33.1	35.1
Q8D	Female labor	15.9	5.9	7.9
Q8E	Available labor	58.1	38.9	37.8
Q8F	Labor costs	36.1	13.1	23.0
Q8G	Available land	24.1	27.9	32.8
City Choice				
Q9A	Labor costs	32.9	13.2	27.2
Q9B	Land costs	28.8	36.1	38.9
Q9C	Good building	59.9	33.2	46.8
Q9D	Airport	36.2	40.0	35.9
Q9E	Highway	59.9	67.2	57.8
Q9F	Headquarters close	10.9	4.2	7.1
Q9G	Other branch close	12.9	11.1	9.9
Q9H	Suppliers	12.8	18.8	13.9
Q9I	Customers	22.1	40.1	33.9
Q9J	Owner's home close	20.1	21.9	20.1
Q9K	City subsidy	1.9	6.8	6.1
Q9L	Quality of life	30.9	18.9	26.9
Q9M	Friendly government	13.2	15.2	10.8
% manufacturing		55.1	67.8	56
Average employment		120.4	121.9	135
Number of Firms		45	72	217

would indicate that this measure does indeed capture the meaning of the underlying variable. For example, the survey asked about the importance of being close to suppliers. The measure used to approximate the availability of suppliers (as well as customers) for the model here was "employment by place of work per square mile." It could be the case that there is no significant difference between the mean of this variable for the cities of firms which answered "yes, suppliers mattered" than the cities of firms that did not say suppliers mattered. This would offer evidence that "employment density" does not adequately reflect the presence of suppliers or customers.

Second, we can investigate what is meant by particular responses to survey questions, and characterize firms which answered yes or no on a set of variables which may suggest better approximations. The survey factors may have meaning for firms beyond what the survey presumes. For example, the survey asked firms about the importance of low-cost labor. Perhaps the "yes" and "no" firms have differences beyond what we might expect—does distance to Loop capture labor costs? Or minority communities? Housing density?

Finally, for a few easily-quantified variables, the findings from such an exercise can attest to the validity of survey responses. For example, did establishments which said highway access was important actually locate near highways?

The Method

This exercise draws on both the survey of 217 branch firms and the municipal database used for the statistical model. A set of variables from the database which in some way measure or are related to the factor in question are chosen, and then the mean of these variables are calculated for "yes" firms and for "no" firms. We can then perform a statistical test to determine whether these means really are that much different from one another (a T-Test for the significance between means).

A city could have contained both firms which said "yes" and firms which said "no" to a particular factor. In this case, the value of the variable for this city was included in the calculation of both means. For example, a firm which chose to locate in Des Plaines city may have said that being close to O'Hare was important, while a second firm did not say proximity to O'Hare was important, but also chose to locate that city. In that case "Des Plaines" variables would be counted in both the "yes" mean and the "no" mean. What is compared is the variable means for all cities in each group.

The Variables

The relevant municipal variables for the 85 cities which had at least one responding firm are described in table 16 (cities without survey returns were not included in this analysis). Many of these variables are those that were

Table 16
Means and Standard Deviations for 85 Cities with Survey Returns

Variable		Mean	Std. Dev.
City demographics and descriptors			
CAVGHSVL	Average housing value	79.3	28.5
CCAPINC	Per capita income	2484.2	654.4
MHSINC	Median household income	25.9	6.5
CPOPDEN	Persons (1,000) per square mile	3.4	2.1
HOUSEDEN	Housing units per square mile	667.9	402.7
CPBLACK	% black population	4.3	9.9
PBLACK	% black city and surrounding cities	6.1	6.4
CITYAGE	Age of city in years	85.1	27.9
Employment in 1980 per square mile			
CMFGDEN8	Mfg employment	576.7	765.7
CTOTDEN8	Total employment	1598.3	1342.0
SMFGDEN8	Mfg emp. city and surrounding	481.5	339.1
STOTDEN8	Total emp. city and surrounding	1439.1	786.1
Distance to central city and transportation variables			
HIGHWAY1 (0,1)	Access ramps to interstate are in city	.49	
HIGHWAY2 (0,1)	Ramp less than 2 miles	.12	
HIGHWAY3 (0,1)	Ramp 2 to 5 miles	.12	
OHARE1 (0,1)	Distance to O'Hare airport: 0 -2 miles	.07	
OHARE2 (0,1)	O'Hare: > 2 miles to 10 miles	.29	
TOLOOP	Distance to Chicago's CBD	27.4	13.2
Labor force (includes the city plus all cities within 5 miles)			
FEM_DEN	Density of women with children	712.4	238.9
MEN_DEN	Density men 18-44	576.1	123.0
ELEM_DEN	Density elementary graduates	575.1	305.1
COL_DEN	Density college graduates	295.7	148.2

used in the municipal database. A few additional ones appear that were left out of the regression models because of multicollinearity or other considerations. In particular, the sections below discuss housing density, per capital income, housing values, and city employment densities in addition to several variables from the statistical models discussed above.

Which Variables Capture Survey Answers?

Table 17(beginning on page 98) presents the relative means on selected variables, by factor, for the group of firms which indicated the factor was important ("YES") and for those who did not ("NO"). Also reported are the significance level for a one-tailed difference-of-means test ("p"), and the count of firms which were in the "yes" and "no" groups (n). The sections to follow use this table to inform us about which statistical variables might be the best measure for different factors we are trying to capture, by referencing the appropriate survey responses. For example, does "distance to downtown" or "average housing value" seem to be a better measure for "quality of life," given the value for cities for firms which said "yes" to "quality of life" versus those that said "no"?

Quality of Life Factors

From table 17, it appears that several measures capture quality of life considerations. Both firms which stated they chose the suburbs versus the central city in search of a better quality of life (Q8A) and firms which indicated that quality of life considerations affected their city choice (Q9L) chose to locate farther from the Loop, not near the airport, and in cities and areas with less industrial development. On average, these firms located in cities 29 miles from Chicago's central business district and in towns with about 1550 workers per square mile, while firms for which these issues were less important were in cities 25 miles away with about 2100 workers per square mile.

What is also interesting is that for firms concerned about "quality of life," avoiding areas with minority populations seems to be part of the concern when choosing the suburbs over the city; yet when choosing among suburbs, minority cities are not avoided by "quality of life" firms. Therefore, it seems as though "quality of life" is sometimes a synonym for a concern about the presence of minority populations and a reason for a suburban location in general.

Other variables usually thought to capture quality of life concerns are not significant. For example, Charney 1983, has suggested that the presence of low-income households is a proxy for quality of life issues. Yet here, firms which checked this factor did not favor towns with higher-income (MHSINC), nor cities with more expensive housing (CAVGHSVL).

Labor Costs

Distance to the central city has been used as a commonly accepted proxy for metropolitan area wage gradients, as wage measures by sub-county area are nearly impossible to obtain. The evidence given here is that this is an acceptable approximation (or at least that firms assume labor costs are lower farther out), while employment density, the presence of college graduates, the presence of women with children, cities with higher incomes, minority populations and older cities might also capture wage differences. Companies which indicated that labor costs concerns affected their choice of the suburbs over the city, and those who said it affected the choice of a particular city, situated themselves farther from downtown Chicago (Q8F and Q9A). Those who wanted lower wages went to towns about 34 miles from the Loop; those who did not located about 10 miles closer.

Firms concerned about their labor costs go to towns with less dense overall development, probably because development indicates a competition for labor and thus a higher wage bill. It is interesting to note that it is total employment and not solely manufacturing employment which appears to drive up wages. These cities also tended to have a smaller percentage of college graduates and more women with children than other towns.

Firms also assumed that minority populations are associated with lower wages. Those who said their choice of the suburbs (Q8F) and of a particular city (Q9A) was influenced by wage considerations tended to choose cities with higher percent black populations. Even though it may merely be the company's *perception* that minorities correlate with lower wages and not in fact the case, it is still interesting to note that firms who wish to pay lower wages will situate themselves in minority communities.

Finally, as expected, companies concerned with their wage bill looked for labor in towns where residents earned less. Median household incomes are lower in towns where these firms went: about $23,000, compared to $27,000 for firms which did not say labor costs were a factor.

Available Labor Force

The question regarding the importance of general labor force availability was only asked regarding the "suburbs rather than city" decision (Q8E). Population density, indicating the general supply of people, is significant, supporting the use of these measure by those such as McGuire 1985 and the use of it here. Industrial development and distance to the central city did not matter.

Two variables regarding *labor characteristics* which matter in this instance are median household income and percent black. Companies who responded "yes" to this factor located in cities with lower median household incomes ($24,500 versus $26,800 for those who said "no"), and higher minority populations, but did not choose places near women with children, or with workers at particular educational levels. Since median household income and minority populations are both also related to labor cost concerns, it probably is the case that firms interpret a survey question regarding "available labor force" as meaning "available, *low-cost*, labor."

Types of Labor: Education Levels and Women

None of our measures seem to reflect the fact that firms were looking for a particular education level (Q8C) or for female labor (Q8D). Neither college nor high school graduates seemed to matter; perhaps a vocational training variable would have fared better. For women, it was neither the presence of women, nor the presence of families with children.

Land and Building Availability and Costs

Question 8G asked establishments whether they chose the suburbs in order to take advantage of available land, while question 9B asked if they chose a particular city because of land cost considerations. Models such as Moses and Williamson (1967), Wasylenko (1980), and McGuire (1985) have used "distance to central business district" to proxy for land costs; and housing density or population density for land availability.

The findings here contend that three measures capture concerns regarding both land costs and land availability. Firms which are concerned with finding available, inexpensive, open land prefer to situate themselves in places farther from the central city. When this is an issue (Q8G), companies on average located 32 miles from the central business district, compared to 24 miles for those for whom it is not. Firms looking for low-cost land, however, do not go as far, an average of just 30 miles. Lower housing values and lower median household incomes are also associated with both land costs and land availability. It is likely that both of these variables measure how welcome industrial and commercial development are to the community (and, by extension, perhaps zoning).

Determinants of Firm Location 93

A fourth measure associated with *land availability* is population density. Population density is a better measure than housing density in terms of capturing land availability. Firms looking for land also avoided locating near O'Hare.[12] A fourth measure associated with *land costs* is the presence of African-Americans. Firms which were looking for low-priced land tended to position themselves in cities with higher minority populations. None of the variables in the database seems to capture building availability.

Transportation Access

Proximity to highways and O'Hare airport were asked about in Q9D and Q9E. While only 9% of the firms which did not say access to O'Hare was important were located less than 2 miles away, fully 37% of those who did want to be near O'Hare were within this distance (OHARE1). As the distance from O'Hare increases, this relationship begins to reverse itself.

For highway access, more firms that said this was important were located in cities with direct access ramps (74% vs. 50% who did not check "highway access"). Note that beyond direct access, mere proximity doesn't seem to matter; cities without direct access but closer to highways than are other cities don't better their chances at capturing more firms needing highway availability (HIGHWAY2 and HIGHWAY3 are not statistically significant).

Unlike the discussions surrounding the other measures discussed so far, the finding of expected relationships for these "access to transportation" probably says more about the validity of survey responses than it does about how to measure difficult-to-quantify variables. Unlike these other variables, "distances to" are easy to calculate and we may be sure that what we are measuring is what we want to measure. However, the fact that these distance measures relate so cleanly to the survey responses does offer evidence for the validity of survey responses.

Access to Customers and Suppliers

A popular indicator of agglomeration economies (the presence of suppliers and buyers) used in regression models is "employment density." The results here, however, indicate that neither total employment nor manufacturing employment per square mile seem to matter to firms looking for proximity to suppliers or buyers. They also did not locate nearer highways or the airport. The extremely odd finding is that those companies looking to locate near suppliers went to cities with *less* development. This may be because these firms went to cities farther from the CBD. One interpretation of this is that firms needing access to suppliers are concerned about *long-distance* suppliers; thus they locate farther from congestion found closer to the central business district. However, companies looking for suppliers also tended to go to older towns. Taken together with distance from the Loop, it may mean that older industrial towns along the metropolitan edge (Elgin, Aurora, Joliet), are more likely to have the kinds of suppliers for which firms are looking.

Proximity to customers, on the other hand, is more of a local issue. Again, employment density does not seem to matter for these firms. Rather, branches which wanted to be near buyers tended to locate somewhat closer to the central city (25 miles vs. 28 miles).

Conclusions

This exercise has suggested that many seemingly hard-to-quantify variables affecting industrial location can be captured by available data. Subjective "quality of life" concerns can be approximated by measures of industrial density, by distance to the central city, and by the presence of minority populations; however housing values and median incomes do not seem to capture this variable. Likewise, several pieces of information commonly used to estimate labor costs and availability seem to be significant: distance to the central city, industrial density, income levels, and the presence of minority populations and women. Land costs are captured by distance to central city, minority populations, median household incomes, and average housing values. Distance to the Loop, median household incomes, and average housing values also approximate land availability; as does population density, and proximity to the airport. Industrial and housing densities do not seem to capture land availability or prices.

In terms of the variables themselves, what is especially surprising is the number of times that distance to the central city proxies for a particular underlying relationship. It seems to measure quality of life concerns, labor costs, available land, land costs, and proximity to suppliers. Population density is variously employed in models as a measure of labor availability and also as an estimate for proxy for land costs. The analysis here seems to indicate that measures of population density better proxy for labor and land availability.

Determinants of Firm Location

Of course, this exercise would not have been possible without assuming the legitimacy of survey responses, even though the validity of answers has often been called into question. That is, for this exercise, the assumption is that when companies stated on the survey that a factor was important, their location choice was influenced by that factor. For example, if a company checked "land costs" on the survey form, this meant that they had obtained data on land prices and chose a city with relatively inexpensive land. Without this assumption, testing the legitimacy of independent variables against these answers would not have been possible. The alternative would have been to presume that survey responses did not reflect firm behavior. In latter case the analysis could have been performed "the other way around": assume that it was the *database* measures which were valid, and then to have checked the validity of questionnaire responses against them. For example, we could have assumed that "distance to central business district" adequately captures land prices, and then examined whether firms which checked this factor on the survey actually went to towns farther from the CBD.

The significance of the distance to transportation variables however, defends the validity of survey responses and thus the decision to test the independent variables against responses seems right. When a firm indicated on the survey form that it was looking for access to highways or airports, its city location reflects this concern. We may conclude that firms did not carelessly check the factor "close to airport"; perhaps the same is true for other survey responses as well.

Table 17
Means and Significance Levels for Difference of Means Tests on Selected City Variables, For Firms Reporting "Yes, Factor was Important" vs. "No"

Quality of Life

Q8A: Suburban Quality of Life

	YES	NO	(p)
OHARE1	.09	.24	.003*
TOLOOP	29.5	25.6	.033*
PBLACK	3.6	5.6	.015*
CPBLACK	4.3	3.6	.581
STOTDEN8	1312.4	1592.8	.003*
SMFGDEN8	421.3	541.4	.004*
CTOTDEN8	1550.2	2138.3	.000*
CMFGDEN8	514.0	828.1	.001*
MHSINC	26.8	25.4	.200
CAVGHSVL	83.8	78.4	.211
CPOPDEN	3.1	3.5	.124
HOUSEDEN	628.8	670.2	.355
n	76	141	

Q9L: City Quality of Life

	YES	NO	(p)
OHARE1	.08	.23	.004*
TOLOOP	29.6	26.0	.086*
PLBACK	4.2	5.1	.314
CPBLACK	4.2	3.7	.703
STOTDEN8	1302.6	1566.3	.009*
SMFGDEN8	406.9	533.9	.002*
CTOTDEN8	1528.5	2083.2	.002*
CMFGDEN8	459.4	814.7	.000*
MHSINC	26.8	25.6	.307
CAVGHSVL	84.2	78.9	.281
CPOPDEN	3.2	3.4	.446
HOUSEDEN	627.3	666.3	.454
n	58	158	

Table 17 continued on next page

Table 17 continued

	Labor		
Q8F: Suburban Labor Costs			
	YES	NO	(p)
STOTDEN8	1170.3	1594.3	.000*
SMFGDEN8	397.8	530.6	.003*
MEN_DEN	642.8	649.3	.242
TOLOOP	33.8	24.9	.000*
CPBLACK	6.6	2.9	.041*
COL_DEN	235.9	333.9	.000*
ELEM_DEN	556.2	507.5	.287
MHSINC	22.9	26.8	.000*
MUNI81	1.2	.98	.035*
CCAPINC	2179.2	2576.7	.000*
CITYAGE	91.7	83.5	.060*
n	51	166	
Q9A: City Labor Costs			
STOTDEN	1187.3	1609.4	.000*
SMFGDEN8	405.9	534.2	.009*
FEM_DEN	760.9	631.9	.001*
MEN_DEN	747.4	729.6	.180
TOLOOP	34.1	24.8	.000*
CPBLACK	6.04	3.0	.057*
COL_DEN	238.0	338.1	.000*
ELEM_DEN	554.4	518.8	.427
MHSINC	23.3	26.9	.000*
NUMI81	1.19	.98	.045*
CCAPINC	2192.1	2591.9	.000*
CITYAGE	92.5	82.8	.017*
n	59	158	
Q8E: Suburban Labor Force Available			
STOTDEN8	1493.6	1495.3	.987
SMFGDEN8	503.0	497.0	.893
FEM_DEN	731.2	717.3	.639
MEN_DEN	709.9	721.7	.673

Table 17 continued on next page

Table 17 continued

	YES	NO	(p)
Q8E: Suburban Labor Force Available (cont.)			
TOLOOP	27.6	26.6	.580
CPBLACK	5.5	2.8	.045*
COL_DEN	302.1	316.4	.445
ELEM_DEN	559.9	535.4	.525
MHSINC	24.5	26.8	.011*
CPOPDEN	3.6	3.2	.055*
n	83	134	
Q8C: Suburban Labor Force Education			
MHSINC	26.3	25.7	.606
FEM_DEN	723.0	727.4	.882
MEN_DEN	716.6	717.4	.977
COL_DEN	306.8	313.1	.729
ELEM_DEN	532.9	551.1	.640
n	76	141	
Q8D: Suburban Female Labor Force			
FEM_DEN	728.2	699.9	.694
n	18	199	
Land			
Q8G: Suburban Available Land			
CPOPDEN	3.1	3.5	.097*
HOUSEDEN	615.8	674.6	.226
STOTDEN8	1388.2	1545.3	.140
SMFGDEN8	490.7	503.4	.782
CAVGHSVL	73.7	83.5	.011*
MHSINC	24.6	26.5	.037*
OHARE1	.13	.218	.093*
HIGHWAY1	.51	.63	.125
TOLOOP	32.3	24.4	.000*
n	70	147	
Q9B: City Land Costs			
CPBLACK	5.4	2.8	.049*
CPOPDEN	3.4	3.3	.895

Table 17 continued on next page

Table 17 continued

Q9B: City Land Costs (cont.)

	YES	NO	(p)
CTOTDEN8	1829.2	1997.5	.375
CMFGDEN8	758.3	692.7	.554
HOUSEDEN	643.7	663.2	.671
TOLOOP	30.3	24.9	.003*
CAVGHSVL	73.4	84.7	.002*
MHSINC	24.5	26.7	.012*
n	84	133	

Q9C: Building Available

	YES	NO	(p)
CPBLACK	2.7	4.8	.068*
CITYAGE	83.8	86.8	.458
TOLOOP	27.6	26.4	.482
CPOPDEN	3.3	3.4	.596
HOUSEDEN	654.5	656.7	.959
CAVGHSVL	82.7	78.2	.262
n	102	115	

Transportation Access

Q9D: Close to Airport

	YES	NO	(p)
OHARE1	.37	.09	.000*
OHARE2	.36	.24	.084*
HIGHWAY1	.74	.50	.000*
HIGHWAY2	.10	.13	.549
HIGHWAY3	.02	.09	.044*
TOLOOP	24.3	28.5	.012*
n	78	139	

Q9E: Close to Highway

	YES	NO	(p)
OHARE1	.216	.152	.228
OHARE2	.344	.206	.023*
HIGHWAY1	.648	.510	.044*
HIGHWAY2	.112	.130	.684
HIGHWAY3	.064	.065	.971
TOLOOP	26.7	27.3	.745
n	125	92	

Table 17 continued on next page

Table 17 continued

Suppliers and Customers	YES	NO	(p)
Q9H: Close to Suppliers			
CPOPDEN	3.4	3.3	.769
STOTDEN8	1212.4	1539.9	.018*
SMFGDEN8	392.3	516.5	.018*
TOLOOP	31.6	26.2	.107
OHARE1	.10	.20	.108
HIGHWAY1	.60	.59	.905
CITYAGE	94.9	83.9	.042*
n	30	187	
Q9I: Close to Customers			
CPOPDEN	3.5	3.0	.102
STOTDEN8	1540.8	1470.7	.501
SMFGDEN8	499.5	499.3	.997
TOLOOP	24.9	28.0	.057*
OHARE1	.162	.203	.459
HIGHWAY1	.65	.56	.203
CITYAGE	84.9	85.7	.867
n	74	143	

*Significant at the 1% level.

NOTES

1. Such associations between variables, called multicollinearity, was assumed to be operating when the correlation coefficients were .70 or higher.

2. FEM_DEN and MEN_DEN are correlated at the .68 level (table 9). Although .68 is below the unofficial "suspect multicollinearity" level of .70, estimations were also performed with each variable separately. In these separate estimates, FEM_DEN remains significant while MEN_DEN is not.

3. The set of 98 was obtained "listwise." As indicated in chapter 3, effective tax rates were obtainable for 108 cities and capital expenditures for 103, but the intersection of these sets (*both* variables) was only 98 places. Although all the cities in this set of 98 had 1980 populations of 10,000 or

Determinants of Firm Location

greater, not all places of 10,000 or greater population had both variables. The cities of 10,000 and more population which were missing one of these variables were: River Grove, Glenwood, Prospect Heights, Round Lake Beach, Hickory Hills, Zion, Blue Island, Villa Park, Bolingbrook, Calumet City, and Berwyn.

4. Because the survey was conceived to be a supplement to the model, where the model is essentially concerned with locations among cities within the suburbs (that is, does not model the choice of the suburbs over other areas), the survey was designed to find out more about why firms chose particular cities rather than why firms chose the suburbs in general. The list of factors offered for the "suburban choice" is therefore fairly short and the discussion thus spends more time on the question "why this particular city?"

5. These four responses for question 7 were: (A) our plant used to be located in Chicago and we wanted to move out of Chicago; (B) our plant used to be somewhere else and we wanted to move to be near Chicago; (C) the headquarters is in Chicago but we wanted to open a branch in the suburbs, and; (D) the headquarters is outside the Chicago area and we wanted to open a branch near Chicago.

6. Data on occupations by gender are taken from the *Geographic Profile of Employment and Unemployment* (U.S. Department of Labor 1990).

7. The answers for the manufacturing plants generally gave less detail and so were less conclusive. "Light manufacturing," "manufacture and assembly," "metal stampings," "manufacturing and distribution," and "typesetting and other pre-press operations" were the typical answers which were less revealing of the occupational nature of the firm than the answers given by business services branches.

8. The occupational analysis in this and later paragraphs is based on answers to question 11 on the firm survey. There is, however, missing data for this question, so that the analysis is based on a subset of 117 firms instead of the 217 returns (including one female-labor firm).

9. Firms choosing female labor were located in Elk Grove Village, Elgin, Hoffman Estates, Elmhurst, Des Plaines, Barrington, Aurora, Burr Ridge, Blue Island, Oak Park, Mundelein, Westmont, Schaumburg, Marengo Joliet Itasca, and two in Lombard.

10. This short analysis is based on 117 responses which included occupational information (that is, occupational data were missing for 100 firms).

11. Although firms which did not choose a particular factor did not explicitly say "no, this factor was *not* important," they are referred to in later paragraphs as "no" firms.

12. Since OHARE1 is a dichotomous variable, the means for the two groups can be interpreted as the proportion of firms located in cities with a value of "1" for OHARE1.

V
Concluding Remarks

The study here support findings in previous studies regarding the variables which influence company location decisions, and, additionally, provide fresh insights on the role of women workers. The following paragraphs first discuss what this study has to say about those factors typically used in location studes. Then disussed is the role of women workers, and implications this study may have for labor markets and economic development efforts.

TYPICAL LOCATION FACTORS

Not surprisingly, traditional location factors such as transportation access, population size, and population density all demonstrated the expected relationship to firm location revealed by previous studies. As have other surveys (McMillan 1965, Schmenner 1980), the importance of transportation access tops the list of factors important to firms making second-stage (local) location decisions. Here, access to highways ranked first, airports fourth, and were even more important to business services firms than to manufacturers. What the model revealed is that direct highway access is most important--firms looking for this mode of transport located in cities with direct access ramps.

Site characteristics also topped the list of important factors in the survey. Such characteristics included building availability and land costs. A finding here not revealed in earlier studies is the difference between manufacturing and business services with regard to their preferred level of site development. Business services firms were likely to want an available building, while manufacturers were more interested in factors pertaining to land. This is supported by the coefficients found in the regression equations, where the business services activity (but not manufacturing) was influenced by capital improvements.

The survey can also shed light on the importance of market characteristics to the second-stage decision. As discussed in chapter 2, it is a tenet of location theory that market factors are considered primarily at the *first* stage. Whatthefindings here suggest is that these previous studies may be biased in terms of primarily investigating manufacturing firms. For this study, 43% of business services stated that access to customers influenced their choice of a particular city.

Not surprisingly, taxes matter. Municipal taxes, available for the full set of 203 cities, dampened the level of manufacturing activity. Effective tax rates was negatively associated with both manufacturing and business services in the 98 cities where this tax measure was available. The difference may be due to the type of cities in which these sectors are likely to be found. Manufacturers may be more likely to cluster in non-residential cities, where the municipal tax rate is closer to the real effective tax rate because of a negligible amount of school district levies. In fact, there is some evidence that manufacturers do so cluster: median household income was negatively related to manufacturing activity but positively related to business services.

The age of a city is a variable new to location studies. This study implies that this variable may be a good choice in terms of capturing the unique characteristics of older industrial towns on the metropolitan fringe: a level of industrial activity which indicates the presence of potential suppliers, appropriate labor force, etc.

WOMEN WORKERS AND FIRM LOCATION

The evidence presented here with regard to labor force factors in general imply that traditional location theory may be mistaken in assuming that labor force characteristics come into play primarily at the first stage decision and are not considered important at the second stage. Clearly, labor researchers in the industrial geography tradition are correct in advocating the primacy of labor considerations for firms at the inter-, and perhaps intra-, city level.

In the study presented here, labor force considerations influenced the municipal choice for a significant number of firms. Business went to cities to generally seek out labor, beyond mere agglomeration effects. The evidence is that firms seek out particular kinds of labor. First, companies looking for low-cost labor tended to be conscious about their decision and went to minority communities, to cities with lower median household incomes, with more second-earner women, older cities, and to cities with fewer college graduates.

Secondly, the presence of women workers affected the level of branch development within a city. We saw that the location of (although not the size of) both manufacturing and business services firms were positively related to the number of women with children in the city and surrounding area. Although only a few branches chose "female labor" in the survey as a reason for choosing the suburbs, firms which were worried about labor force factors in general tended to hire more women. Although "female labor" was chosen by just a few, the fact that the variable was significant in the regression equation implies that, even if they did not consciously seek out such labor, women *are* ultimately employed by these firms and act as an inducement to their location.

Third, the branches which did state that they chose the suburbs in order to employ women were likely to be back office branches. These firms tended to employ more clerical workers than the average for their industry. This confirms findings by Nelson (1986) that the presence in the suburbs of second-earner, primarily white, female workers who prefer a short commute has acted as an inducement particularly to branch operations to choose suburban locations.

IMPLICATIONS FOR DEVELOPMENT AND LABOR

The importance of labor force characteristics in general suggests that those who advocate a "labor-force-based" approach to economic development are correct in assuming that development potential may be affected by labor availability. This strategy suggests that a good economic development strategy must start with a consideration of local labor force potential in order to yield the best results. If, as is demonstrated here, labor considerations are so important to firms, then the economic development potential of localities will depend upon the attributes of the local "labor landscape." Some of these attributes are amenable to state and local development strategies, such as education and job training. Other attributes such as ethnicity and gender, are not so.

This has implications for the economic potential of particular places, and adds knowledge to what we know about the economic competition between cities and their suburbs. What factors come into play in the decentralization of economic activity? We can add labor considerations to the list of site attributes, such as land availability and site assembly costs, on which city development departments have traditionally focused. If some labor attributes, such as gender and ethnicity, are not amenable to local development strategies, this suggests other courses of action for central city development efforts. Metropolitan revenue-sharing strategies, reverse commuting, and the like are all suggested.

In addition, the strategy of the part of firms to locate branches in suburban areas, has repercussions for the structure of labor markets. If firms disaggregate internal functions across space then internal career ladders will be truncated by spatial barriers. Employees in branch firms can be promoted, but when the next promotion means a longer commute to a headquarters establishment it may create a obstacle, especially for women with household responsibilities. These responsibilities may preclude a longer commute to another city or downtown location.

The effect of disaggregating firm functions across space in this manner will be evident in the earnings and occupational structure of the labor market in the aggregate. It will be more difficult for workers to "move up the ladder" internally and, one resul may be that the labor force will consist of two classes--"branch" workers and "headquarter" workers with earnings and occupations reflecting this hierarchy. In fact, since the mid-1970s, a bifurcation of earnings has been evident in the U.S. economy. The earnings distribution has come to resemble an "hourglass" shape, reflecting the shrinking of the middle class. What this study does is to suggest that *space* plays a role in creating and reinforcing this segmentation.

In addition, as a consequence of this, the effect will be recursive. That is, if firms spatially disaggregate internal functions, and career ladders are truncated, then one result will be to reinforce the segregation of labor across space.

Appendix 1

Table 18
Municipalities Included in the Study

	Census City Name	# Firms	Employment	1990 Population (1,000)
1	Elk Grove village	57	6532	33.4
2	Schaumburg village	55	5012	68.6
3	Des Plaines city	54	5860	53.2
4	Oak Brook village	43	3276	9.2
5	Aurora city	36	7649	99.6
6	Rolling Meadows city	35	9119	22.6
7	Franklin Park village	34	6673	18.5
8	Lombard village	32	4021	39.4
9	Elgin city	30	5540	77.0
10	Naperville city	28	10974	85.4
11	Addison village	26	1645	32.1
12	Melrose Park village	24	7494	20.9
13	Northbrook village	24	2536	32.3
14	Arlington Heights village	23	4864	75.5
15	Joliet city	23	6263	76.8
16	Downers Grove village	22	3019	46.9
17	Bensenville village	21	1816	17.8
18	Chicago Heights city	21	4598	33.1
19	Elmhurst city	20	3600	42.0
20	St. Charles city	20	2371	22.5
21	West Chicago city	20	25	14.8

Table 18 continued on next page

Table 18 continued
Municipalities Included in the Study

	Census City Name	# Firms	Employment	1990 Population (1,000)
22	Wheeling village	19	2479	29.9
23	Itasca village	17	1330	6.9
24	Wood Dale city	17	1052	12.4
25	Batavia city	16	3043	17.1
26	Skokie village	16	9702	59.4
27	Lisle village	14	2222	19.5
28	Mount Prospect village	14	1637	53.2
29	Schiller Park village	14	1494	11.2
30	Waukegan city	13	2184	69.4
31	Bridgeview village	12	1407	14.4
32	Crystal Lake city	12	1641	24.5
33	Hinsdale village	12	1184	16.0
34	La Grange village	12	2976	15.4
35	South Holland village	12	1149	22.1
36	Wheaton city	12	1064	51.5
37	Deerfield village	11	3763	17.3
38	Evanston city	11	701	73.2
39	Mundelein village	11	1512	21.2
40	Glenview village	10	2725	37.1
41	Rosemont village	10	376	4.0
42	Villa Park village	10	624	22.2
43	Hillside village	9	1153	7.7
44	Hoffman Estates village	9	788	46.6
45	Westmont village	9	1533	21.2
46	Blue Island city	8	976	21.2
47	Gurnee village	8	1309	13.7
48	Harvey city	8	566	29.8
49	Lemont village	8	361	7.3
50	Palatine village	8	574	39.2
51	Park Ridge city	8	943	36.2

Table 18 continued on next page

Table 18 continued
Municipalities Included in the Study

	Census City Name	# Firms	Employment	1990 Population (1,000)
52	Barrington village	7	998	9.5
53	Geneva city	7	1126	12.6
54	Harvard city	7	940	6.0
55	Lockport city	7	540	9.4
56	Morton Grove village	7	3500	22.4
57	Westchester village	7	325	17.3
58	Woodstock city	7	666	14.3
59	Burr Ridge village	6	822	7.7
60	Carol Stream village	6	1001	31.7
61	Carpentersville village	6	405	23.0
62	Huntley village	6	1174	2.5
63	Libertyville village	6	1970	19.2
64	McHenry city	6	940	16.2
65	Maywood village	6	833	27.1
66	Park Forest village	6	976	24.7
67	Plainfield village	6	806	4.6
68	Bellwood village	5	1552	20.2
69	Broadview village	5	651	8.7
70	Dolton village	5	721	23.9
71	Montgomery village	5	4121	4.3
72	North Chicago city	5	625	35.0
73	Oak Lawn village	5	301	56.2
74	Oak Park village	5	1075	53.6
75	Thornton village	5	245	2.8
76	Alsip village	4	267	18.2
77	Cary village	4	650	10.0
78	Countryside city	4	200	5.7
79	Glen Ellyn village	4	320	24.9

Table 18 continued on next page

Table 18 continued
Municipalities Included in the Study

	Census City Name	# Firms	Employment	1990 Population (1,000)
80	Highland Park city	4	167	30.6
81	Homewood village	4	175	19.2
82	Matteson village	4	171	11.3
83	Oak Forest city	4	462	26.2
84	Roselle village	4	159	20.8
85	Summit village	4	565	10.0
86	Wauconda village	4	246	6.3
87	Zion city	4	355	19.8
88	Bartlett village	3	307	19.4
89	Bolingbrook village	3	285	40.8
90	Buffalo Grove village	3	603	36.4
91	Calumet city	3	200	37.8
92	Frankfort village	3	955	7.2
93	Grayslake village	3	690	7.4
94	Lake Zurich village	3	443	14.9
95	Lansing village	3	228	28.1
96	Lincolnshire village	3	790	4.9
97	Lyons village	3	1598	9.8
98	Mokena village	3	92	6.1
99	Northlake city	3	315	12.5
100	River Grove village	3	160	10.0
101	Vernon Hills village	3	221	15.3
102	Warrenville city	3	575	11.3
103	Wilmington city	3	860	4.7
104	Berkeley village	2	210	5.1
105	Bloomingdale village	2	620	16.6
106	Crest Hill city	2	83	10.6
107	Forest Park village	2	106	14.9
108	Fox Lake village	2	50	7.5
109	Glendale Heights village	2	85	28.0

Table 18 continued on next page

Table 18 continued
Municipalities Included in the Study

Census	City Name	# Firms	Employment	1990 Population (1,000)
110	Hazel Crest village	2	47	13.3
111	Lake Bluff village	2	70	5.5
112	Lake Forest city	2	90	17.8
113	Long Grove village	2	330	4.7
114	Marengo city	2	295	4.8
115	North Aurora village	2	528	5.9
116	Round Lake village	2	3520	3.6
117	South Chicago Heights village	2	165	3.6
118	South Elgin village	2	65	7.5
119	Sugar Grove village	2	70	2.0
120	West Dundee village	2	175	3.7
121	Western Springs village	2	830	12.0
122	Wilmette village	2	500	28.7
123	Algonquin village	1	25	11.7
124	Antioch village	1	21	6.1
125	Berwyn city	1	52	45.4
126	Channahon village	1	158	4.3
127	Chicago Ridge village	1	29	13.6
128	Clarendon Hills village	1	25	7.0
129	Crestwood village	1	250	10.8
130	Darien city	1	33	18.3
131	Dixmoor village	1	41	3.6
132	Flossmoor village	1	120	8.6
133	Fox River Grove village	1	170	3.6
134	Glenwood village	1	29	9.3
135	La Grange Park village	1	30	12.9
136	Orland Park village	1	35	35.7
137	Palos Park village	1	100	4.2
138	Phoenix village	1	25	2.5
139	Posen village	1	30	4.2

Table 18 continued on next page

Table 18 continued
Municipalities Included in the Study

Census	City Name	# Firms	Employment	1990 Population (1,000)
140	River Forest village	1	55	11.7
141	Riverside village	1	170	8.8
142	Romeoville village	1	700	14.1
143	Steger village	1	120	8.6
144	Tinley Park village	1	33	37.1
145	Willow Springs village	1	26	4.5
146	Winfield village	1	30	7.1
147	Winnetka village	1	250	12.2
148	Woodridge village	1	75	26.3
149	Worth village	1	570	11.2
150	Barrington Hills village	0	0	4.2
151	Braidwood city	0	0	3.6
152	Brookfield village	0	0	18.9
153	Burbank city	0	0	27.6
154	Burnham village	0	0	3.9
155	Country Club Hills city	0	0	15.4
156	Crete village	0	0	6.8
157	Deer Park village	0	0	2.9
158	East Dundee village	0	0	2.7
159	Ford Heights village	0	0	4.3
160	Glencoe village	0	0	8.5
161	Hanover Park village	0	0	32.9
162	Hawthorn Woods village	0	0	4.4
163	Hickory Hills city	0	0	13.0
164	Highwood city	0	0	5.3
165	Hometown city	0	0	4.8
166	Indian Head Park village	0	0	3.5
167	Inverness village	0	0	6.5
168	Island Lake village	0	0	4.5
169	Justice village	0	0	11.1

Table 18 continued on next page

Table 18 continued
Municipalities Included in the Study

Census	City Name	# Firms	Employment	1990 Population (1,000)
170	Kenilworth village	0	0	2.5
171	Kildeer village	0	0	2.5
172	Lake Barrington village	0	0	3.9
173	Lake in the Hills village	0	0	5.9
174	Lake Villa village	0	0	2.9
175	Lindenhurst village	0	0	8.0
176	Lynwood village	0	0	6.5
177	Markham city	0	0	13.1
178	Midlothian village	0	0	14.4
179	New Lenox village	0	0	9.6
180	Northfield village	0	0	4.6
181	North Riverside village	0	0	6.0
182	Olympia Fields village	0	0	4.2
183	Orland Hills village	0	0	5.5
184	Palos Heights city	0	0	11.5
185	Palos Hills city	0	0	17.8
186	Park city	0	0	4.7
187	Peotone village	0	0	2.9
188	Prospect Heights city	0	0	15.2
189	Richton Park village	0	0	10.5
190	Riverwoods village	0	0	2.9
191	Robbins village	0	0	7.5
192	Round Lake Beach village	0	0	16.4
193	Round Lake Park village	0	0	4.0
194	Sauk Village village	0	0	9.9
195	Shorewood village	0	0	6.3
196	Sleepy Hollow village	0	0	3.2
197	South Barrington village	0	0	2.9
198	Stickney village	0	0	5.7
199	Stone Park village	0	0	4.4

Table 18 continued on next page

Table 18 continued
Municipalities Included in the Study

Census	City Name	# Firms	Employment	1990 Population (1,000)
200	Streamwood village	0	0	31.0
201	University Park village	0	0	6.2
202	Willowbrook village	0	0	8.6
203	Winthrop Harbor village	0	0	6.2

Appendix 2
Survey Questionnaire

Note: The survey in its original format was only two pages long (front and back of one page).

1. *Business Name (Printed on questionnaire when sent)*
2. City and Zip Code

   _____

3. Could you describe what kind of work is done at this plant?

   _____

4. About how long has this plant been in this city?

   _____

5. Are you the person to whom this questionnaire was addressed?
                       A. Yes   B. No

5a. Were you involved in choosing the city where your plant is now located?
                       A. Yes   B. No

6. Did your branch relocate from somewhere else or was this a new facility?
A. We relocated from _____
(city and state)
B. This was a new facility

7. Why did your company decide to locate this plant in the Chicago suburbs?
A. Our plant used to be located in Chicago and we wanted to move out of Chicago.
B. Our plant used to be somewhere else and we wanted to move to be near Chicago.
C. The headquarters is in Chicago but we wanted to open a branch in the suburbs.
D. The headquarters is outside Chicago and we wanted to open a branch near Chicago.

8. What was attractive about the suburbs *in general*? Please circle all that apply.
A. Quality of Life (schools, churches, etc.)
B. Close to another branch.
C. Labor supply: Good education/skill levels
D. Labor supply: Good female labor force
E. Labor supply: Availability
F. Labor supply: Costs
G. Lots of available land
H. Other _____

Appendix 2 - The Survey Questionnaire

9. What was attractive about this particular city? Choose all that apply.
A. Costs: Labor
B. Costs: Land
C. Good building available
D. Close to airport
E. Close to highway
F. Close to headquarters
G. Close to other branch
H. Close to suppliers/materials
I. Close to customers
J. Close to manager/owners home
K. Received a city subsidy
L. Quality of Life (schools, churches, etc.)
M. Friendly city government
N. Other reason

10. About how many people are employed here?

11. Please fill in the following table, telling us what percent of your workforce fits into each of the eight categories. The total of the eight boxes should equal 100%. If you don't know percents, just fill in the numbers.

	Male	Female	Don't Know
Professional/Managers			
Technical			
Production			
Clerical/Support			

12. How often do employees get promoted from this branch to a job at another branch or the headquarters?
A. Very Often
B. Frequently
C. Sometimes
D. Not Often
E. Don't Know
F. This question doesn't apply to my plant.

13. Is there anything else you would like to add that we didn't ask you about?

THANKS FOR YOUR TIME

References

Aldrich, Howard, Arne Kalleberg, Peter Mardsen and James Cassell. 1989. In Pursuit of Evidence: Sampling Procedures for Locating New Businesses. *Journal of Business Venturing* 4 (November): 367-86.

American Map Corporation. 1993. *Chicagoland Six County Atlas*. Wood Dale, Illinois: American Map Corporation.

Anderson, Donald and Stephen A. Johnston. A Linkage Approach to Identifying Industrial Location. *Growth and Change* 23 (Summer): 21-34.

Bartik, Timothy J. 1985. Business Location Decisions in the United States: Estimates of the Effects of Unionization, Taxes and Other Characteristics of States. *Journal of Business & Economic Statistics* 3 (January) 14-22.

___. 1991. *Who Benefits From Sate and Local Economic Development Policies?* Kalamazoo, MI: W.E. UpJohn Institute for Employment Research.

Birch, David L. 1987. *Job Creation in America*. New York: The Free Press.

Blair, John P. and Robert Premus. 1987. Major Factors in Industrial Location: A Review. *Economic Development Quarterly* 1 (January): 72-85.

Carlson, Virginia L. 1995. Identifying Neighborhood Businesses: A Comparison of Business Listings. *Economic Development Quarterly* 9 (February): 50-59.

Carlton, Dennis W. 1979. Why New Firms Locate Where They Do: An Econometric Model. In *Interregional Movements and Regional Growth*, ed. William Wheaton, 13-50. Washington, DC: The Urban Institute.

———. 1983. The Location and Employment Choices of New Firms: An Econometric Model with Discrete and Continuous Endogenous Variables. *Review of Economics and Statistics* 65 (August): 440-49.

Census of Population and Housing. 1980. Summary Tape File 3 (Illinois) [machine- readable data files]. Prepared by the Bureau of the Census.

Washington: The Bureau [producer and distributor], 1981. Special extract prepared for The Federal Reserve Bank of Chicago by the University of Illinois Chicago Area Geographic Information Study, 1993.

Charney, Alberta H. 1983. Intraurban Manufacturing Location Decisions and Local Tax Differentials. *Journal of Urban Economics* 14 (May): 184-205. New York: John Wiley and Sons.

Chicago Tribune-Rand McNally. 1992. *Chicagoland Map.* Chicago: Chicago Tribune.

Cornia, G.,W. Testa, and F. Stocker. 1978. *State-Local Fiscal Incentives and Economic Development.* Urban and Regional Development Series Number 4. Columbus, OH: Academy for Contemporary Problems.

Dillman, Don A. 1978. *Mail and Telephone Surveys: the Total Design Method.*

England, Kim V. L. 1993. Suburban Pink Collar Ghettos: the Spatial Entrapment of Women?. *Annals of the American Association of Geographers* 83 (May): 225-242.

Epping, G. Michael. 1982. Important Factors in Plant Location in 1980. *Growth and Change* 13 (April): 47-51.

Erickson, Rodney A. and Michael Wasylenko. 1980. Firm Relocation and Site Selection in Suburban Municipalities. *Journal of Urban Economics* 8 (January): 69-85.

Forkenbrock, David J. And Norman S. J. Foster. 1996. Highways and Business Location Decisions. *Economic Development Quarterly* 10 (3): 239-248.

Fortune, Inc. 1977. *Facility Location Decisions.* New York: Fortune, Inc.

Fox, William F. 1981. Fiscal Differentials and Industrial Location: Some Empirical Evidence. *Urban Studies* 18 (February): 105-11.

Garreau, Joel. *1991. Edge City: Life on the New Frontier.* New York: Doubleday.

Gottlieb, Paul D. 1995. Residential Amenities, Firm Location and Economic Development. *Urban Studies* 32 (9):413-431.

Greenhut, Melvin L. 1956. *Plant Location in Theory and Practice: The Economics of Space.* Chapel Hill: University of North Carolina Press.

Hanson, Susan and Geraldine Pratt. 1995. *Gender, Work, and Space.* New York: Routledge.

Hanson, Susan and Geraldine Pratt. 1992. Dynamic Dependencies: A Geographic Investigation of Local Labor Markets. *Economic Geography* 68 (October): 373-405.

Hanson, Susan and Geraldine Pratt. 1991. Job Search and the Occupational Segregation of Women. *Annals of the Association of American Geographers* 8 (2): 229-253.

Hastings, Steven E. and Frank M. Goode. 1982. Improved Measures of Industrial Location Factors. *Growth and Change* 13 (January): 25-31.

Illinois, Secretary of State. 1991. *Illinois Counties & Incorporated Municipalities: May 1, 1991*. Illinois: Secretary of State.

Illinois, Department of Revenue. 1981. *Tax Rates for Illinois Taxing Districts*. Illinois: Department of Revenue.

Illinois, Department of Employment Security 1979, 1991. *Where Workers Work in the Chicago Metropolitan Area* (Chicago: Illinois Department of Employment Security, 1979 and 1991).

Isard, Walter. 1975 *Introduction to Regional Science*. Englewood Cliffs, N.J.: Prentice-Hall.

Johnson, Merril. 1991. An Empirical Update on the Product-cycle Explanation and Branch-plant Location in the Nonmetropolitan US South. *Environment and Planning A* 23 (March): 397-409.

Johnston-Anumonwo, Ibipo. 1997. Race, Gender, and Constrained Work Trips in Buffalo, NY, 1990. *The Professional Geographer* 49 (3): 306-317.

Kieschnick, Michael. 1981. *Taxes and Growth: Business Incentives and Economic Development*. Washington: Council of State Planning Agencies.

Kriesel and Kevin T. McNamara. 1991. A County-level Model of Manufacturing Plant Recruitment with Improved Industrial Site Quality Measurement. *Southern Journal of Agricultural Economics* 23 (July): 121-27.

Lopez, Rigoberto A. and Nona R. Henderson. The Determinants of Location Choices for Food Processing Plants. *Agribusiness* 5 (December): 619-32.

Losch, August. 1954. *The Economics of Location*. New Haven: Yale University Press.

MacDonald, Heather and Alan Peters. 1994. Spatial Constraints on Rural Women Workers. *Urban Geography* 15 (8): 720-740.

Massey, Doreen. 1973. Towards a Critique of Industrial Location Theory. *Antipode* 5 (January): 33-39.

___.1978. Capital and Locational Change: The UK Electrical Engineering and Electronics Industries. *The Review of Radical Political Economics* 10 (3): 39-54.

___.1984. *Spatial Divisions of Labor: Social Structures and the Geography of Production.* New York: Methuen.

Massey, Doreen and Nancy A. Denton.. 1993. *American Apartheid: Segregation and the Making of the Underclass.* Cambridge, MA: Harvard University Press.

McDonald, John F. 1984. *Employment Location and Industrial Land Use in Metropolitan Chicago.* Champaign, Illinois: Stipes Publishing.

McGuire, Therese J. 1985. Are Local Property Taxes Important in the Intrametroplitan Location Decisions of Firms? An Empirical Analysis of the Minneapolis-St. Paul Metropolitan Area. *Journal of Urban Economics* 18 (July) 226-34.

McHone, W. Warren. 1986. Supply-Side Considerations in the Location of Industry in Suburban Communities: Empirical Evidence from the Philadelphia SMSA. *Land Economics* 62 (February): 64-73.

McMillan, Thomas E., Jr. 1965. Why Manufacturers Choose Plant Locations. *Land Economics* 41 (August): 239-46.

Mills, Edwin S. 1972. *Studies in the Structure of the Urban Economy.* Baltimore, Md: Johns Hopkins Press.

Moses, Leon and Harold F. Williamson, Jr. 1967. The Location of Economic Activity in Cities. *American Economic Review, Papers and Proceedings* 57 (May): 211-22.

Mueller, Eva and James N. Morgan. 1962. Location Decisions of Manufacturers. *American Economic Review, Papers and Proceedings* 52 (May): 204-17.

Muth, Richard F. 1969. *Cities and Housing: the Spatial Pattern of Urban Residential land use.* Chicago: University of Chicago Press.

Nelson, Kirsten. 1986. Labor Demand, Labor Supply and the Suburbanization of Low-Wage Office Work. In *Production, Work, Territory: The Geographical Anatomy of Industrial Capitalism*, ed. Allen J. Scott and Michael Storper, 149-169. Boston: Allen Unwin.

Oakland, William H. 1978. Local Taxes and Intraurban Industrial Location: A Survey. In *Metropolitan Financing and Growth Management Policies: Principles and Practices*, ed. George F. Break, 13-30. Madison: University of Wisconsin Press.

Oksanen, E.H. and J.R. Williams. 1984. Industrial Location and Inter-Industry Linkages. *Empirical Economics* 9 (April): 139-50.

Peck, Jamie. 1989. Reconceptualizing the Local Labor Market: Space, Segmentation, and the State. *Progress In Human Geography* 13 (January): 42-61.

Persky, Joseph J., Wim Wiewel, and Elliot D. Sclar. 1991. *Does American Need Cities: An Urban Investment Strategy for National Prosperity*. Washington, D.C.: Economic Policy Institute.

Schmenner, Roger W. 1975. City Taxes and Industry Location. Ph.D. diss, revision, Yale University.

――. 1978. *The Manufacturing Location Decision: Evidence from Cincinnati and New England*. Washington: U.S. Department of Commerce, Economic Development Administration.

――. 1980. *The Location Decisions of Large Multiplant Companies*. Washington: U.S. Department of Housing and Urban Development.

――. 1982. *Making Business Location Decisions*. Englewood Cliffs, N.J.: Prentice-Hall.

Schmenner, Roger W., Joel C. Huber and Randall L. Cook. 1987. Geographic Differences and the Location of New Manufacturing Facilities. *Journal of Urban Economics* 21 (January): 83-104.

Scott, Allen J. 1988. *Metropolis: From the Division of Labor to Urban Form*. Los Angeles: University of California Press.

Scott, Allen J. and Edward Soja. 1996. *The City: Los Angeles and Urban Theory at the End of the Twentieth Century*. Berkeley: University of California Press.

Stafford, Howard A. 1974. The Anatomy of the Location Decision: Content Analysis of Case Studies. In *Spatial Perspectives on Industrial Organization and Decision-making*, ed. F. E. Ian Hamilton, 169-187. New York: John Wiley & Sons.

Storper, Michael and Richard Walker. 1983. The Theory of Labour and the Theory of Location. *International Journal of Urban and Regional Research* 7 (January): 1-41.

U.S. Department of Commerce, Bureau of the Census. 1982 Census of Population and Housing, 1980: Summary Tape File 1A [machine readable data files]/ prepared by the Bureau. Washington, D.C.: Bureau of the Census.

Wasylenko, Michael. 1980. Evidence of Fiscal Differential and Intrametropolitan Firm Relocation. *Land Economics* 56 (August): 339-349.

Weber, A. 1929. *Theory of the Location of Industries*. Chicago: University of Chicago Press.

Index

A
access
  to airports, 52, 71, 82
  to customers, 82-83, 93
  to highways, 52, 68, 82
  to labor, 21
  to markets, 4-5
  to suppliers, 87, 93
  to transportation, 31, 88, 93
age of cities, 54, 72
agglomeration economies, 4, 21-22, 28, 93
airport access, 71, 82
Aldrich, Howard, 41
Anderson, Donald, 26
availability
  for building, 82, 92-93
  of energy, 28
  of input, 33
  of labor, 19, 20-21, 25, 81-82, 91-92
  of land, 66, 81, 83, 92-93
  of workers, 16, 25, 81-82

B
backward linkages, 26
Bartik, Timothy, 5, 15, 18-19, 23, 27-29
Birch, David, 41
Blair, John, 34

branches, 14, 15, 22-23
  activity of, 46
  and markets, 33
  and taxes, 29
  employment by municipality of, 45
  identification of, 41
  importance of location, 9
  model of activity of, 47
  prediction of activity of, 75
  Standard Industrial Classification Code of, 43
building availability, 82, 92-93
business services, prediction of, 74

C
Carlson, Virginia, 41
Carlton, Dennis, 14, 15, 18, 22-23, 25-29
chance factors, 34
Charney, Alberta, 15, 21, 27, 32, 35, 90
Chicago
  employment in, 9-10
  inner-ring of, 10
  metropolitan area of, 41
  outer-ring of, 10-11
  transportation improvements of, 11

cities
  age of, 54, 74
  variables of, from samples and responding firms, 63
college graduates, 58
commuting distances, 20
consequences of development, 57
Cook, Randall, 5, 15, 18-19, 23, 25, 28-29, 34-35
Cornia, G., 5
correlation coefficients, 69-70
customer access, 82-83, 93

D
Denton, Nancy, 8
dependent variables, model of, 47
development, consequences of, 57
disaggregated analysis, 27
disposition of surveys, 60
distances
  and firm locations, 31
  and land price, 32
  commuting, 20
  to central business district, 53
DMI listings. see Dun's Market Indicators
Dun's Market Indicators, 41

E
economics, factors of surrounding area, 49
economies, agglomeration, 4, 21-22, 28, 93
education levels, 92
  density of, 74
effective tax rates, 56, 77
elementary school graduates, 59
employment
  density, 54-55, 88, 93
  growth, 27
  in Chicago, 9-10
  levels of, 46
  prediction of levels, 75
Epping, G., 15
Erickson, Rodney, 6, 15, 20, 22, 24, 26-27, 30-31, 49

F
female workers. see women workers
firms
  economic activity of, 41
  inter suburban moves of, 80
  number of by municipality, 44
  relocation of, 13, 20
  types of, 24
first stage decisions, 5, 14, 83
  and energy availability, 28
  and market factors, 32
  and quality of life factors, 34
  importance of workers in, 18
  labor force factors in, 18
forward linkages, 26
Fox, William, 30

G
Garreau, Joel, 3
gender, 58
  density of, 74, 77
geographic stages of decisions, 5
Goode, Frank, 27
Gottlieb, Paul, 34-35
graduates
  college, 58
  elementary school, 59
Greenhut, Melvin, 4, 32

H
Hanson, Susan, 7, 15, 20, 24-25
Hastings, Steven, 27
Henderson, Nona, 15, 24, 27, 29, 33

Index

highway access, 52, 68, 82
household incomes, 72
Huber, Joel, 5, 15, 18-19, 23, 25, 28-29, 34-35

I
important factors
  by industry type, 81
  levels for difference of, 96-100
independent variables
  model of, 47-48
industrial location theory, 3-4
industrial patterns, 6
inner-ring of Chicago, 10
input
  availability of, 33
  linkages, 26, 73
  supply, 27
inter-municipality decisions. *see* second stage decisions
inter-state decisions. *see* first stage decisions
inter-suburban moves, 80
intra-metropolitan
  differences, 31
  location decisions, 7
Isard, Walter, 34

J
Johnson, Merril, 15, 18, 23, 29-30, 33
Johnston, Stephen, 26
Johnston-Anumonwo, Ibipo, 8

K
Kieschnick, Michael, 14-15, 18, 23, 33
Kriesel, 15, 20-22, 24, 31

L
labor, *see also* workers
  accessibility of, 21
  availability of, 19, 20-21, 25, 81-82, 91-92
  characteristics of, 7
  climate of, 19
  costs of, 91
  kinds of, 25
  potential supply of, 57
  productivity of, 18-19, 25
  rates, 19-20
land
  area, 21, 50, 56
  availability of, 81, 83, 92-93
  costs, 66, 82, 93
  price and site attributes, 32
  use intensity of, 31-32
linkages, forward and backward, 26
locations
  economic reasons for, 4
  intra-metropolitan decisions for, 7
  prediction of, 75
  studies (table), 15
Lopez, Rigoberto, 15, 24, 27, 29, 33
Losch, August, 4

M
MacDonald, Heather, 8
manufacturing
  and employment, density of, 73
  and services, prediction of, 74
markets, access to, 4, 5
Massey, Doreen, 6, 8
McGuire, Therese, 6, 15, 20-22, 27, 30, 92
McHone, W. Warren, 30
McMillan, Thomas, 5, 15, 20, 29-30

McNamara, Kevin, 15, 20-22, 24, 31
median household income, 54
minority populations, 53, 72, 90-91
Morgan, James, 15, 18-19, 23, 29, 34
Moses, Leon, 15, 27, 31, 92
movement of jobs, 3
Mueller, Eva, 15, 18-19, 23, 29, 34
municipal capital expenditures, 57, 77
municipal conditions, true measure of, 77
municipal database, 39-40, 88
municipal tax rates, 56

N
Nelson, Kirsten, 3, 7, 8, 15, 23

O
Oakland, William, 30
Oksanen, E.H., 26
optimal firm location, economic reasons for, 4
outer-ring of Chicago, 10-11
output demand, 27
output linkages, 26, 73

P
percent of population based variables, 57
Persky, Joseph, 8
Peters, Alan, 8
population density, 50, 66, 77, 91
potential labor supply, 57
Pratt, Geraldine, 7, 15, 20, 24, 25
Premus, Robert, 34
production hours, 27
property tax rates, 55
proximity to airport, 52, 71, 82

Q
qualitative factors, 75
quality of life factors, 33-34, 81-82, 90

R
reduced form equation, 77
regression coefficients, 67-68, 79
  reduced form, 78
relocation, 80
residual terms, 76
reverse commuting, 8
right-to-work laws, 5, 16, 20, 35

S
Schmenner, Roger, 5-6, 9, 14-15, 18-20, 22-25, 27-35
Sclar, Elliot, 8
second stage decisions, 5, 14, 20-21, 80, 83
  and energy availability, 28
  and quality of life factors, 34
  and site attributes, 30-31
  and taxes, 28-29
  importance of workers in, 18
  labor force factors in, 18
single-site firms, 14-15, 22-23
  and markets, 33
  and taxes, 29
spatial division of labor, 6
Stafford, Howard, 15, 18-19, 29, 33-35
Standard Industrial Classification (SIC) codes, 26, 43
statistical models, 14, 15-17, 20, 26, 30, 39
statistical studies
  and market factors, 33
  and taxes, 29
statutory tax rates, 55

Stocker, F., 5
suburban cities, economic base for, 8-9
suppliers
  access to, 87, 93
  long distance, 94
survey responses
  female labor importance, 85
  of women workers employed, 87
  means and standard deviations of, 89
surveys, 14-17, 22-23, 27, 39-40
  administration of, 59
  and energy, 28-29
  and personal factors, 34
  development of, 59
  disposition of, 60
  returns of, by industry, 61

T
tax rates, 5, 73
  and branches, 29
  and industry location, 30
  and second stage decisions, 28-29
  and single-site firms, 29
  and statistical studies, 29
  municipal, 56
  property, 55
  statutory, 55
Testa, W., 5
total employment, density of, 72
transportation
  access to, 31, 83, 93
  costs of, 4
  improvements in Chicago, 11
type of work, 83-84

V
variables
  descriptive statistics for, 51
  percent of population-based, 57

W
wages, 19, 20, 21, 23
Wasylenko, Michael, 6, 15, 20, 22, 24, 26-27, 29-31, 49, 92
Weber, A., 4
Wiewel, Wim, 8
Williams, J.R., 26
Williamson, Harold, 15, 27, 31, 92
women workers, 23-24
  commute constraints of, 8
  occupational niches of, 8
workers, *see also* labor
  availability of, 16, 25, 81-82
  characteristics of, 6, 84
  factors of, 17, 23
  geographically specific, 7
  measuring importance of, 17
  mobility of, 6